Maine
Shipwrecks, Treasures, Pirates

By Ted Burbank

Salty Pilgrim Press
www.SaltyPilgim.com

ISBN 978-1-935616-06-1

All rights reserved. No part of this book may be reproduced in any form without written permission from Salty Pilgrim Press excepting brief quotations for book reviews.

For additional copies or more information, please contact:

Salty Pilgrim Press
17 Causeway Street
Millis, MA 02054 USA
1 508 794-1200
captain@saltypilgrim.com

Second Edition

Copyright © 2013 by Theodore P Burbank

Cover design by G. Scott B.
Sunshine Joy
Woonsocket, RI

Cover photo by Jason Song

Printed in the USA

Forward

Shipwrecks
Shipwrecks and the rocky coast of Maine are almost synonymous. Hundreds, if not thousands of ships, and their crews, have met their end in the icy cold waters of the Maine coast. We have listed hundred of shipwrecks from Kittery to Quoddy Light and tell the stories of many. It is therefore quite natural to expect a book titled "Shipwrecks on the Maine Coast."

Pirates
It is less likely however, to see a title such as "Pirates and Treasure in Maine." It is not usual to associate pirates with Maine – pirates were in the warm Caribbean – not in the foggy, cold waters of Maine – or were they?

We have chronicled for you the many pirates, famous and not so famous, that have plied the coast of Maine for centuries. Who were the pirates of Maine? Why were they here? What might they have left behind, and why?

Treasure
Tales of where the pirates have buried their loot and places where some of it has been found are told in these pages. Has all the treasure been found?

Gold, Silver and Jewels were not only buried by pirates but by merchant, farmers and others all over Maine. Why? - Because banks and other institutions were either not available, or not trusted.

There's gold in them there streams! Yes, gold and valuable gems can be found in some of Maine's many streams and other locations. You may be surprised how accessible the valuable deposits are. We tell you where you might begin your search and find your own treasure.

Table of Contents

Treasure in Maine	1
Why did pirates bury their treasure?	2
What you should know about pirates	3
Pirates Elect the Captain	4
Articles of Agreement, or Pirate's Code	5
Sample Articles of Agreement	6
Punishment	7
History of Piracy	8
Disability Pay	9
Pirate Myths	10
Ships of the Era	12
Pirate Weapons	15
Other Names Meaning Pirate	16
The Spanish Main	17
The Brass Monkey debate	18
Meet the Pirates	19
Captain Samuel Argall	20
Captain Dixie Bull	21
Captain Kidd	22
More Bad Luck	23
Letter of Marque has Name Wrong	24
Kidd's Admission of Buried Treasure Ignored	26
Treasure Ship Map	27
Bad Luck Streak Continues	28
Black Sam Bellamy	29
The Saga of Maria "Goody" Hallett	31
His lover is a witch	32
Goody Swallowed by a Whale	33
Goody Hallet poem	34
The Beginning of Bellamy's Career	35
Legend of Buried Treasure on Cape Cod	38
Was Bellamy Tricked into Eternity?	39
Whydah Discover off Wellfleet	40
George and Rachel Wall	41

Captain Sandy Gordon	42
Blackbeard	44
Blackbeard's buried treasure	46
Jack Quelch	50
Edward Lowe	51
Philip Ashton	53
William Fly	54
Paulgrave Williams	56
John King – the youngest pirate	59
Richard Nolan	61
Hendrick Quintor	62
John Phillips	63
Where treasure may be found	65
Isle of Shoals	66
Sandy Gordon's White Island Treasure	70
Rubies of Boon Island	75
Treasures in Casco Bay	77
Mantinicus Island	78
Pond Island	82
Orrs Island	83
Johns Island	84
Penobscot Bay	85
Bucksport Area	86
Circus Ship Treasure	87
Treasure in Boothbay	88
Mid Coast treasure	89
Machias region treasure	90
Allagash region treasure	92
Inland treasure	93
Carpenter Ridge Diamonds	95
Native and Natural treasure	97
Mother Lode of Gold – Southern Maine	98
Finding Relics and Old Coins	99
Finding Treasure on Beaches	100
15 Best Treasure Hunting Sites	101
Where to Find Gold in Maine	102

More Places to Find Gold	103
How to Pan for Gold	104
The Mechanics of Panning for Gold	105
Mineral & Gem Collecting Places	106
Rangley Area Gold and Platinum	107
Verona Island Gold Mine	108
More lost treasures	109
Benedict Arnold's Gold	110
South Coast wrecks – where and when	111
Isles of Shoals Area	112
Isles of Shoals Shipwrecks	113
South Coast to Casco Bay	114
Details and stories	121
Nottingham Galley – 1710	122
Ghosts of the Wreck Sagunto	123
Edyth Ann – 1865	124
Samuel J Goucher – 1911	125
USCG Leader – 1919	126
Twin Wrecks at Cape Porpoise	127
The Wandby – 1921	128
USS Squalus (SS-192) – 1939	129
USS 0-9 (SS70) - 1941	130
The Skottland – 1942	131
The William H Machen – 1943	132
The Empire Knight – 1944	133
USS Eagle 56 (PE-56) - 1945	134
Gruesome Tale of a Christmas Day Shipwreck	135
Cape Elizabeth to Casco Bay – where and when	139
South Coast Details and Stories of Wrecks	145
Steamer Bohemian – 1864	146
Schooner, Mary Alice – 1869	147
Steamer, Cambridge	148
The Anne C Maguire – 1886	149
The Susan P Thurlow – 1897	150
The Edward J Lawrence – 1925	151
Steamer, Bay State – 1916	152

Cabin, Cruiser Don – 1941	153
USS S-212 (SS-126) – 1945	155
Freighter, Oakley L Alexander – 1947	156
Freighter, SS Novadoc – 1947	158
Mid Coast and Penobscot Bay – where and when	159
Listing of Wrecks – Boothbay to Penobscot Bay	160
Stories and Tales – Mid Coast and Penobscot Bay	171
Pinnace, Little James - 1624	172
Galleon, Angel Gabriel - 1635	173
The Industry – 1700	174
USS Adams – 1814	175
The Royal Tar – 1836	176
The Georgia – 1875	177
Steamer, City of Portland – 1884	178
Tug, Cumberland	179
The A H Whitmore – 1903	180
Tug, D T Sheridan – 1924	181
S S Roosevelt	182
Battle for New Ireland	183
The Penobscot Expedition – 1779	184
The Battle for New Ireland	187
Penobscot Expedition's Order of Battle	188
Battle of Hampton	191
The Aroostook War of 1842	192
Ships lost in the Battle for New Ireland	193
Colonial Vessels Lost in the Battle for New Ireland	194
The British Side of the Story	196
Remains of a 1779 Ship	197
Shipwrecks on the Bold Coast	199
Shipwrecks Mt Desert and Downeast - where & when	200
Machiasport Shipwrecks	207
Stories and Tales Mount Desert and Downeast	209
Wreck of the Grand Design	210
HMS Halifax – 1775	213
The New York – 1826	214

Schooner, Neptune's Bride – 1860	215
Bar Harbor Ferry Boat Disaster – 1899	216
Ferry, Cimbria – 1899	218
The Alice M Davenport – 1902	219
Schooner, Annie Gus – 1905	222
Great Storms on the Coast of Maine	223
The Storm of 1842	224
Portland Gale - 1898	228
42 Maine Vessels lost to the Storm	231
Resources	235
Other books by the author	239

Treasure in Maine

All along the Maine coast are more islands than can be counted, and many of these have been suggested as sites for buccaneers and privateers such as Captain Kidd, Captain Bellamy, and their ilk to have buried treasure. Those most often mentioned are listed below.

Why Were Pirates in Maine?

What were pirates doing in Maine waters anyway? Why weren't they in the warm waters of the sunny Caribbean instead?

Answer - Pirates of the day were adventurers primarily from Europe; England and Ireland in particular. That be why me pirate speak be a lot like me Irish accent, *ahhaa!* They were usually just passing through on their way home along with their bounty.

As we shall see Captain Kidd, perhaps the most often referenced Maine pirate, was not the only pirate to ply the waters off Maine's rocky shores. A few other infamous pirates raiding off the coast of Maine include **Blackbeard, Samuel Bellamy, Dixie Bull, Jack Quelch, William Fly, Rachel Wall, and Ned Low** and many more

Some of Captain William Kidd's gold and silver could have been buried anywhere on the coast or on one of Maine's countless islands such as: **Mt. Desert Island, Oak Island or Squirrel Island** off Boothbay Harbor or perhaps **Jewel Island** or perhaps somewhere along the shore of the **Kennebec River** probably near **Gardiner or Hallowell.** Other reports have his some of his treasure hidden near the coastal town of **Machias**.

If and when any Pirate treasure is found, most probably it will consist primarily of **Spanish-American** coins, although there is the possibility that some **Massachusetts silver** could be included.

Why Did Pirates Bury Their Treasure?

Actually, pirates seldom would bury their gold, silver, jewelry and other valuables. In reality, pirates burying treasure was rare. Most often explanation as to why pirates buried their treasure was that they were being pursued by "the law" and would off load the booty to return and get it when "the coast was clear."

The pirate known to actually have buried treasure was William Kidd. He is reported to have buried some of his wealth at various places along the New England coast. He hoped that his treasure could serve as a bargaining chip in negotiations in charges that he engaged in pirating.

Who were the Pirates in Maine?

The very first pirate in the New World was Captain Dixie Bull who in 1632 began pirating, primarily in Penobscot Bay. Over the next few hundred years others would follow including: John Rhodes, Thomas Pound, Thomas Tew, John Quelch, Ned Lowe, William Kidd, Blackbeard, Paulgraves Williams and "Black" Sam Bellamy

Captain Kidd's Buried Treasure

There is more buried treasure attributed to Captain Kidd than to any other pirate. Kidd's treasure is reported to be buried at: Block, Patience, Hope, Conanicut and Hog islands in Rhodes Island, Charles and the Thimble islands in Connecticut, Gardiner and Long islands and various islands in the Hudson in New York, Plum Island and Cape Cod in Massachusetts, Isles of Shoals off Maine and New Hampshire, Penobscot Bay Islands and elsewhere along the Maine coast and Oak Island in Nova Scotia. Some of his booty actually has been uncovered, the largest stash being found on Gardiner Island off Long Island and south of Cape Cod

What You Should Know About Pirates

Democratic societies were the exception during the 'Golden Age of Piracy' (seventeenth and eighteenth centuries).

Europe was ruled by aristocratic kings and queens whose whims were the law. Similarly, the commands of a captain at sea were undisputable, and any infraction or deviation was met with harsh penalties.

Sea captains were known to be extremely brutal and often fed their crews rotten and maggot infested foods. Sailors frequently suffered from scurvy and other nutrition depravation-based disorders. Many crew members were aboard because they had been forcibly conscripted into service. The horrid living conditions and brutality of the captain and his officers caused many sailors of the day to develop a severe intolerance for absolute authority.

Pirates Elected Their Officers and Captain

A pirate ship functioned as a democracy with each crewman having an equal vote concerning operation of the ship. The crew had the power and the right to replace their leaders for any reason.

A major exception to this rule by mutual agreement was during battle when the captain's word was the undisputable law and any deviation from his command could result in death. The following is an excerpt from a pirate's trial in 1721 in London's Old Bailey. "They choose a captain from amongst themselves, who in effect held little more than that title, excepting in an engagement, when he commanded absolutely and without control. At all other times, the captain heeded the wishes of his crew."

Some suggest that portions of the pirate ship's model of a democratic society can be found in America's constitution. The most exact example could be the U.S. President becoming Commander in Chief of all the armed forces in times of war.

The ship's quartermaster was the officer with the real power over the commerce of the ship when not in battle. It was the quartermaster who kept the records of the booty and who was in charge of assuring its fair distribution amongst the crew. He, therefore, had to be trusted and respected by the crew. He also had to be somewhat educated as the position required that he posses the ability to read, write and compute.

Articles of Agreement or Pirate's Code

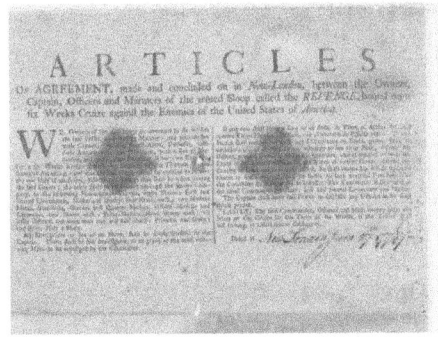

Life aboard a pirate ship was governed by rules originally called the Chasse-Partie or Charter Party and later referred to as Articles of Agreement, or Code of Conduct. All hands were required to sign on before they could join the crew.

To become a full-fledged member of the crew each person was required to sign or make his mark plus swear an oath of allegiance. The swearing ceremony usually involved a Bible; however, crossed pistols, swords or a human skull were known to be used as well.

When a ship was captured, its crew members could elect to sign on as full-fledged members of the crew and share equally in the booty. Some would refuse and be pressed or be forced to be pirates anyway. However, if captured they would not be found guilty of piracy because they had not signed the articles.

Sample Pirate's Articles of Agreement

The Captain is to have two full Shares; the Master is to have one Share and a half; the Doctor, Mate, Gunner & Boatswain, one Share and a quarter.

    I.   Every man shall have an equal vote in affairs of moment. He shall have an equal title to the fresh provisions or strong liquors at any time seized, and shall use them at pleasure unless a scarcity may make it necessary for the common good that a retrenchment may be voted.

    II.   Every man shall be called fairly in turn by the list on board of prizes, because over and above their proper share, they are allowed a shift of clothes. But if they defraud the company to the value of even one dollar in plate, jewels or

	money, they shall be marooned. If any man rob another he shall have his nose and ears slit, and be put ashore where he shall be sure to encounter hardships.
III.	None shall game for money either with dice or cards.
IV.	The lights and candles should be put out at eight at night, and if any of the crew desire to drink after that hour they shall sit upon the open deck without lights.
V.	Each man shall keep his piece, cutlass and pistols at all times clean and ready for action.
VI.	No boy or woman to be allowed amongst them. If any man shall be found seducing any of the latter sex and carrying her to sea in disguise he shall suffer death.
VII.	He that shall desert the ship or his quarters in time of battle shall be punished by death or marooning.
VIII.	None shall strike another on board the ship, but every man's quarrel shall be ended on shore by sword or pistol in this manner. At the word of command from the quartermaster, each man being previously placed back to back, shall turn and fire immediately. If any man do not, the quartermaster shall knock the piece out of his hand. If both miss their aim they shall take to their cutlasses, and he that draweth first blood shall be declared the victor.

No man shall talk of breaking up their way of living till each has a share of f1,000. Every man who shall become a cripple or lose a limb in the service shall have 800 pieces of eight from the common stock and for lesser hurts proportionately.

IX	The captain and the quartermaster shall each receive two shares of a prize, the master gunner and boatswain, one and one half shares, all other officers one and one quarter, and private gentlemen of fortune one share each.
X	The musicians shall have rest on the Sabbath Day only by right. On all other days by favour only.

These were the Articles of Captain George Lowther, & his company

Punishment

Below is a list of the punishments metered out to pirates at their trial at Nijenburg in 1763 revealing the severity of the penalties at the time.

Sentenced to breaking on the wheel; hanged.

Sentenced to breaking on the wheel; broken on the wheel.
Sentenced to 3 times keelhauling, 200 lashes, and public humiliation; 3 times keelhauled, 200 lashes, banished.
Sentenced to death; 3 times keelhauled, 200 lashes, publicly humiliated.
Sentenced to death; thrown 3 times from the main mast, 150 lashes, banished.
Hanged, then beheaded.

Sentenced to hanging; lashed, burn-marked, lost his wage, banished.

Sentenced to breaking on the wheel and strangulation. His corpse was not allowed a burial.

Sentenced to hanging; was lashed, branded, and received 25 years of forced labour.

Beheaded.

Hanged, then beheaded.

Notice that rehabilitation is not on the list.

History of Piracy

The history of piracy dates back more than 3,000 years, but its accurate account depends on the actual meaning of the word 'pirate'. In English, the word piracy has many different meanings and its usage is still relatively new. Today, some uses of the word have no particular meaning at all. A meaning was first ascribed to the word piracy sometime before the XVII century. It appears that the word pirate (peirato) was first used in about 140 BC by the Roman historian Polybius.

The Greek historian Plutarch, writing in about 100 A.D., gave the oldest clear definition of piracy. He described pirates as those who attack without legal authority not only ships but also maritime cities. Piracy was described for the first time, in Homer's "The Iliad" and "The Odyssey". For a great many years there remained no unambiguous definition of piracy. Norse riders of the 9th and 11th century AD were not considered pirates but rather were called "Danes" or "Vikings". Another popular meaning of the word in medieval England was "sea thieves". The meaning of the word pirate most closely tied to the contemporary was established in the XVIII century AD. This definition dubbed pirates "outlaws" whom even persons who were not soldiers could kill. The first application of international law actually involved anti-pirate legislation. This is due to the fact that most pirate acts were committed outside the borders of any country.

Sometimes governments gave rights to the pirates to represent them in their wars. The most popular form was to give a license to a private sailor – privateer to attack enemy shipping on behalf of a specific king. Very often a privateer when caught by the enemy was tried as an outlaw notwithstanding the license.

Pirate's Disability Pay

There is no argument that a pirate's job was indeed a hazardous one. To lose a limb, an eye or otherwise become disabled and, therefore no longer be an able bodied seaman, was a definite possibility. Some would claim they preferred a swift death over a debilitating disability. Compensation amounts by type of injuries are shown below. These were very sizable and generous amounts in the 1700s.

In pieces of eight

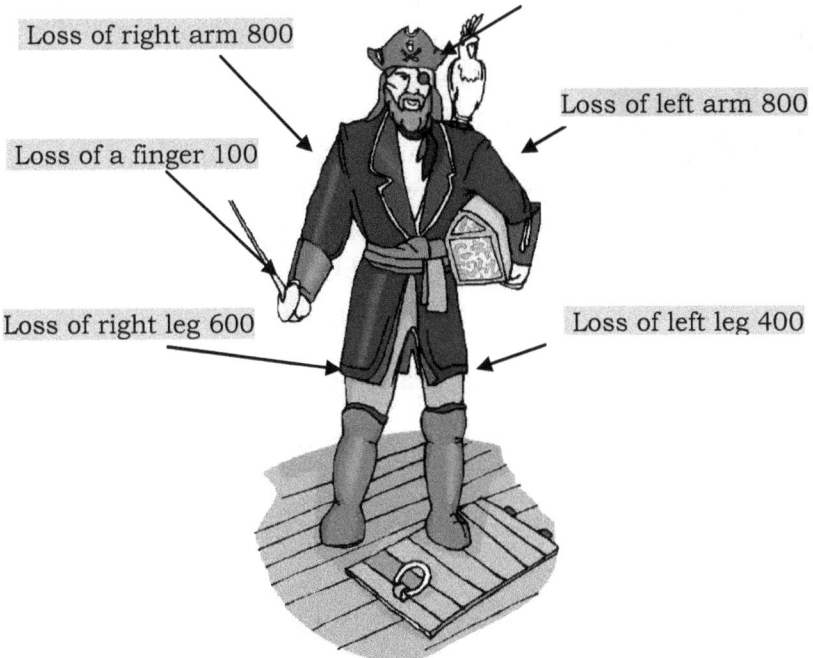

- Loss of an eye 100
- Loss of right arm 800
- Loss of left arm 800
- Loss of a finger 100
- Loss of right leg 600
- Loss of left leg 400

Disability payments would be made from the gross booty, and the individual shares would then be computed from the remainder. Injured pirates were given non-physically demanding work such as cooking meals, operating cannons, and washing the ship decks. They still were entitled to receive a normal share even though they were disabled and capable of limited participation.

Pirate Myths

Pirate Hooks:

Hooks were probably not as prevalent as one might imagine. Some attribute the popularity of pirates armed with hooks to the story "Peter Pan" that starred the pirate character Captain Hook.

Undoubtedly pirates did loose hands during their bloody battles. The few who might survive such a severe wound, given the level of medical prowess aboard the typical pirate ship, could have had such a device crafted by the ship's carpenter.

More likely he would bleed to death before the battle was over and medical attention rendered.

Parrots:

The genesis of the pirate and the parrot legend probably is the story "Treasure Island", specifically the character "Long John Silver". There is a good deal of debate on this subject as many expect that pirates were much too busy to permanently station a parrot upon their shoulder.

This legend becomes more unlikely as pirates at sea for long periods were more likely to prefer fresh meat over the companionship of a messy bird.

Peg Legs:

Popularity of this image probably originates from the story "Treasure Island", and the character "Long John Silver". Although there is basis for this image it is surely overdone.

When a pirate suffered a severe wound to the leg, as many were prone to do, the only option to save his life was amputation of the gangrened or infected limb. This job was usually given to either the ship's cook or carpenter as surgeons aboard pirate ships were uncommon.

As you might suspect few "operations" were successful. Those that did survive would, in addition to using crutches, often fashion a substitute limb out of available materials which most commonly was wood.

Ships of the Era

Here is a sampling of ships on the seas during the Golden Age of Piracy :

Brig – Brigantine - a two masted ship, square rigged on both masts. The two ship types showed more variance in the 19th century. It was a popular choice of many pirate crews, carried as many as 10 cannon and had a crew of one hundred.

Frigate - name used for a variety of ships but formalized by the English in the late 17th century to mean a vessel smaller than a ship of the line. Carried 24-38 guns with three fully rigged masts, their speed made them well suited to convoy duty and hunting pirates.

Galleon - This was the ship of choice for the Spanish during the 16th through 18th centuries. It was 100-150 feet long, 40-50 feet wide and carried 600 tons or more. Usually had three masts and was square rigged with a lateen sail on the mizzenmast and

two to three gun decks

Schooner: This 100 ton, with 8 cannon and a crew of 75 was a favorite amongst pirates because it was fast and shallow drafted. This meant they could easily catch slower moving cargo ships and, easily hide in shoal waters and coves to avoid capture by deep drafted "Man of Wars."

Sloop –Very popular with pirates because of its shallow draft and speed, capable of up to 11 knots, could carry up to 75 crew and mounted 14 cannon.

Naval Sloop: This was a pirate hunting ship. Armed with 12 nine pound cannons this 65 foot, 113 ton ship with a crew of 70 was dreaded by pirates. It was a very fast boat and the 7 pairs of oars allowed them to chase pirates even in windless conditions.

Merchant Ship: The name given to most commercial ships in the late 17th and early 18th centuries. This 80 foot, 280 ton ship manned by a crew of about 20 was referred to by seamen as a "Carrier." They were quite fast and could be armed with as many as 16 guns.

Dutch Flute: Very popular in the early 17th century as a cargo ship because this 300 ton, 80 foot ship was inexpensive to build and could be sailed with a crew of only 12. Because she carried half again as much cargo as similar ships, the Flute became the ship of choice of maritime interests and pirates alike.

Pirate Weapons

Cannon – demi–cannon was a naval gun (French for half cannon) which fired a solid shot ranging in weight from 11lbs to 36lbs

Cannon Shot – Cannons fired more than just cannon balls. Grape Shot - Iron balls, each the size of a tennis ball, bound in a canvas bag.

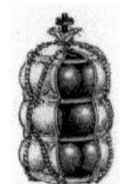

Chain Shot - Heavy balls joined by a chain designed to tangle and tear down rigging and masts

Canister Shot - Cylindrical cases containing pistol balls, used at close range to kill people

Carcass Shot – A flaming mistle filled with highly flammable matter, designed to set ships on fire.

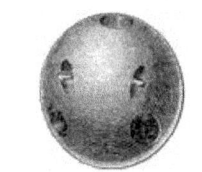

Blunderbuss pistol - A short pistol of wide bore and flaring muzzle. It fires multiple balls at once. This made the blunderbuss the ideal weapon for boarding ships

Other Names Meaning Pirate

Privateer - A ship privately owned and crewed but authorized by a government during wartime to attack and capture enemy vessels and accordingly, a privateer was supposedly not to be tried for piracy. Essentially a pirate was a self-employed soldier paid only by what he plundered from an enemy.

Buccaneer - The buccaneers were first hunters of pigs and cattle on the island of Hispaniola. They were driven off by the Spanish and turned to piracy therefore, the term originally referred to privateers who fought against the Spanish. Later it referenced sailors of the Atlantic, specifically the Caribbean. Buccaneers had a reputation of being heavy drinking, cruel sailors.

French settlers in the Caribbean who used to barbecue or "smoke" wild boar and oxen were called buccaneers. A *boucan* or *buccan* is the name for a wooden framework on which meat was. Boucanier literally means "someone who makes smoke".

Marooners - Marooner is a corruption of the Spanish word "cimarrona" which loosely translates to "deserter" or runaway. These deserters or runaways fell into two groups:

- Spanish sailors who deserted their ship to escape the brutal treatment metered out by the Spanish navy and
- Cimmaron Negroes. These were the run away of slaves that had been brought to the Americas by Spain to haul the gold

More names for a pirate:

Brethren of the Coast,
Brotherhood of the Coast,
On the Account,
Gentleman of Fortune,
Sea Dog,
Freebooter,
Corsair,
Sea-wolf,

The Spanish Main

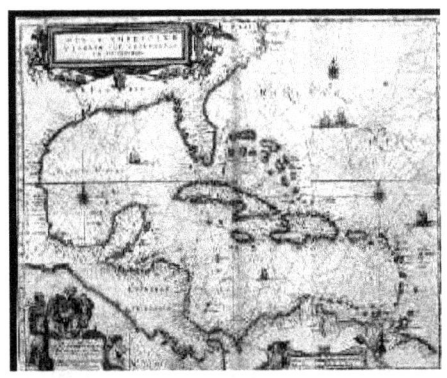

The New World coast from the top of South America through the Caribbean to Northern Florida was known as "The Spanish Main" *(left)*. It was from ports along these coasts that large Spanish treasure ships sailed for Europe and upon which pirates and privateers preyed.

Outfitting warships ships was an expensive proposition for any government. In the 1700 and 1800s fleets of private ships were employed by governments to conducted war against their enemies as agents of the state.

Letters of Marque

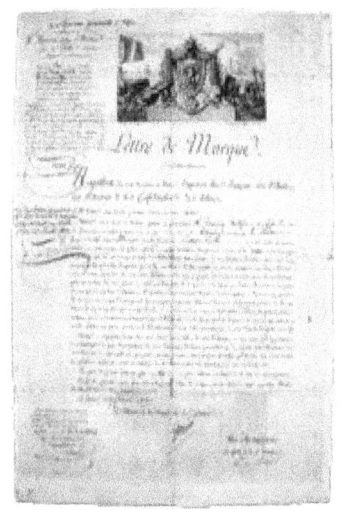

Letter of Marque

These "Privateers' would be issued "Letters of Marque" that entitled a private ship to attack the enemy's ships. The privateers would split any booty captured with the nation's treasury as a sort of payment for being granted a license to steal. Both the men and their ships were referred to as "privateers."

Even the U.S. Constitution of 1787 authorized the issuance of Letters of Marque. By the middle of the 1800s, various conventions and treaties in Europe effectively put an end to the issuance of the letters and the Golden Age of Piracy

.

The Brass Monkey and Cold Weather Debate

The story: In the heyday of sailing ships, all war ships and many freighters carried iron cannons. Those cannons fired round iron cannon balls. It was necessary to keep a good supply near the cannon, but they had to find a way to prevent them from rolling about the deck.

The best storage method devised was a square based pyramid with one ball on top, resting on four resting on nine which rested on sixteen. Thus, a supply of 30 cannon balls could be stacked in a small area right next to the cannon.

There was only one problem; how to prevent the bottom layer from sliding or rolling from under the others. The solution was a metal plate called a "Monkey" with 16 round indentations. But, if this plate was made of iron, the iron balls quickly would rust to it. The solution to the rusting problem was to make "Brass Monkeys."

Few landlubbers realize that brass contracts much more and much faster than iron when chilled. Consequently, when the temperature dropped too far, the brass indentations would shrink so much that the iron cannon balls would come right off the monkey.

Thus, it was quite literally, "Cold enough to freeze the balls off a brass monkey." (And all this time, you thought that was an improper expression, didn't you?)

Rebuttal: This explanation appears to be a legend of the sea without historical justification. In actuality, ready service shot was kept on the gun or spar decks in shot racks (also known as shot garlands in the Royal Navy) which consisted of longitudinal wooden planks with holes bored into them, into which round shot (cannon balls) were inserted for ready use by the gun crew.

Meet the Pirates

Captain Samuel Argall
Dixie Bull
Captain William Kidd
"Black" Sam Bellamy
Edward Teach a/k/a Blackbeard
Jack Quelch
Ned Lowe
William Fly
Joe Bradish
Palgrave Williams
Thomas Pound
George and Rachael Welch
Philip Ashton (not a Pirate)
Captain Sandy Gordon

Captain Samuel Argall (1572-1641)
Captured Pocahontas

He was a buccaneer and later knighted by the king. He is said to have buried a rich treasure in the seventeenth century in the Isles of Shoals, off Portsmouth, New Hampshire,
In 1609, Argall was the first to determine a shorter northern route from England across the Atlantic Ocean to the Virginia Colony based at Jamestown.

In 1610 captain Samuel Argall named the Delaware River and Bay for the governor of Virginia, Thomas West, 3rd Baron De La Warr. The state of Delaware takes its name from the river and bay.

In 1613 on a voyage up the Potomac, Argall captured Pocahontas, the daughter of Chief Powhatan. Argall took her to Jamestown and held her as a hostage for English prisoners held by her father.

Commanding an English ship for the Virginia Company while deputy governor of Virginia, he enters Frenchman's Bay, Maine, contesting the French claim to Acadia. Argall fired the first shot killing the Jesuit Gilbert du Thet and seriously wounded four others. Two men were drowned. He captured and plundered the French ships and took 15 citizens back to Virginia in chains.

On 26 June, 1622, he was knighted by King James I. In 1625 he was named admiral for New England with a fleet of 28 vessels with which he took many prizes. Argall was never married. He died at sea on or about 24 January, 1626.

Pirate Captain Dixie Bull

Dixie Bull (or **Dixey Bull**) was an English sea captain, and the first pirate known to prey on shipping off the New England coast, especially Maine. A native of London, he came to Boston in 1631 and started sailing the Maine coast with a small vessel and traded with the Indians.

In 1632, while traveling in the Penobscot Bay area, he was attacked by a roving band of French in a small pinnace. It is also possible that he was present in Castine Harbor when a French force attacked the trading post there.

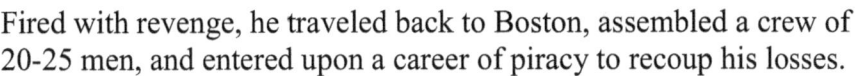

Whatever the details, his ship was captured and all his trade goods and provisions confiscated.

Fired with revenge, he traveled back to Boston, assembled a crew of 20-25 men, and entered upon a career of piracy to recoup his losses.

His fame as the "Dread Pirate" derived from his attack in 1632 on the settlement of Pemaquid which was then center of the lucrative fur trade in Maine. Few pirates had the temerity to attack a defended town. Sailing into the harbor, with what is said to be three ships, he opened fire on the stockade there and sacked the town.

Some stories say he joined the French, others that he returned to England, and still others that he was hanged in Tyburn. Legend says that he buried treasure on Damariscove Island and Cushing Island in Casco Bay. Others have him at Cape Cod's Wellfleet Harbor.

The legend of Dixie Bull was soon enshrined in ballads; the most famous of them being "The Story of Dixie Bull" and "The Slaying of Dixie Bull". This ballad describes a duel between Dixie Bull and a fisherman from Pemaquid, Daniel Curtis on an island near that town, in which Dixie Bull was killed, saving the town.

Capt. William Kidd –
The Bad Luck Kidd

Kidd was born in 1645 into a respectable family at Greenock, Scotland. He had settled in New York and was a successful sea captain. In 1695, at the age of 49, the governor of New York and Massachusetts, Richard Coote, enlisted Kidd's aide in reducing the piratical activities of such infamous pirates as Thomas Tew, John Ireland and Thomas Wake as well as any enemy French shipping. Thus William Kidd's career began as a privateer and not as a pirate. In fact, we shall see that Captain Kidd was never a pirate at all!

Kidd purchased a new vessel, hardly something a real pirate would do, that he named *Adventurer*. It was a galley of 284 tons which he equipped with thirty four cannon. He then recruited a sizeable crew of only the finest sailors of the day.

Bad luck found Kidd almost immediately – while in mid-ocean the British navy stopped his vessel and "recruited" most of Kidd's handpicked mariners thereby forcing him back to shore to replenish his now depleted crew.

Unfortunately, because the Royal Navy had immediately preceded him, the only sailors left represented a miserable mix of former pirates and hardened criminals. Bad luck again, but Kidd forged ahead confident in his abilities to accomplish his goals.

He set to sea once more only to have a sudden and ghastly attack of cholera decimate and kill more than a third of his crew. This bit of bad luck caused Kidd to remain at anchor while he again went ashore to find replacements for his dead crewmembers. This last bit of luck, however, had a positive aspect. While at anchor Kidd discovered fatal flaws in his new ship's construction, flaws that certainly would have caused the *Adventurer* to sink in the first storm it encountered while at sea.

Intent upon completing his mission, Kidd stole a French ship and immediately began his quest to capture pirates and French shipping. More bad luck – Try as they might, not a pirate or French ship could they find. Therefore, by the end of 1697, the crew was becoming restless and mutiny was in the air. Kidd finally agreed to attack any non-English vessel, not just French or pirate ships.

More Bad Luck

Captain Kidd returned to New York after a year of successful privateering only to find he had been betrayed by his backers and the governor. He was now a wanted man and charged with piracy.

Kidd, using his lawyer as intermediary, negotiated with the governor in Boston for safe entry into the city. Bad luck and deceit – again he was betrayed, this time by his own lawyer, and he and his motley crew were thrust into Stone Prison to await trial as pirates.

More than a year later, most of which time Kidd spent in solitary confinement, Captain Kidd was sent to England to be tried for piracy upon the high seas and murder. His pleas for clemency in letters to King William III, allegedly one of the backers, were ignored. On May 23rd, 1701, he was hanged at Execution Dock in London.

Even his Letter of Marque had his name wrong!

This Letter of Marque was granted to one Captain <u>Robert</u> Kidd who is believed to actually be Captain William Kidd as it was issued contemporaneously and with the same charge issued by Governor Richard Coote.

William Rex,
William the Third, by the grace of God, King of England, Scotland, France and Ireland, defender of the faith, &c. To our trusty and well beloved Capt. Robert Kidd, commander of the same for the time being,

Greeting: whereas we are informed, that Capt. Thomas Too, John Ireland, Capt. Thomas Wake, and Capt. William Maze or Mace, and other subjects, natives or inhabitants of New-York, and elsewhere, in our plantations in America, have associated themselves with divers others, wicked and ill-disposed persons, and do, against the law of nations, commit many and great piracies, robberies and depredations on the seas upon the parts of America, and in other parts, to the great hindrance and discouragement of trade and navigation, and to the great danger and hurt of our loving subjects, our allies, and all others, navigating the seas upon their lawful occasions.

Now know ye, that we being desirous to prevent the aforesaid mischiefs, and as much as in us lies, to bring the said pirates, free-booters and sea-rovers to justice, have thought fit, and do hereby give and grant to the said Robert Kidd, (to whom our commissioners for exercising the office of Lord High Admiral of England, have granted a commission as a private man-of-war, bearing date the 11th day of December, 1695,) and unto the commander of the said ship for the time being, and unto the officers, mariners, and others which shall be under your command, full power and authority to apprehend, seize, and take into your custody as well the said Capt. Thomas Too, John Ireland, Capt. Thomas Wake and Capt. Wm. Maze or Mace, as all such pirates, free-booters, and sea-rovers, being either our subjects, or of other nations associated with them, which you shall meet with upon the seas or coasts, with all their ships and vessels, and all such merchandizes, money, goods, and wares as shall be found on board, or with them, in case they shall willingly yield themselves; but if they will not yield without fighting, then you are by force to compel them to yield.

And we also require you to bring, or cause to be brought, such pirates, free-booters, or sea-rovers, as you shall seize, to a legal trial, to the end they may be proceeded against according to the law in such cases. And we do hereby command all our officers, ministers, and other our loving subjects whatsoever, to be aiding and assisting to you in the premises.

And we do hereby enjoin you to keep an exact journal of your proceedings in execution of the premises, and set down the names of such pirates, and of their officers and company, and the names of such ships and vessels as you shall by virtue of these presents take and seize, and the quantities of arms, ammunition, provision, and lading of such ships, and the true value of the same, as near as you can judge.

And we do hereby strictly charge and command you, as you will answer the contrary at your peril, that you do not, in any manner, offend or molest our friends or allies, their ships or subjects, by colour or pretence of these presents, or the authority thereby granted.

In witness whereof, we have caused our great seal of England to be affixed to these presents.
Given at our court in Kensington, the 26th day of January, 1695, in the 7th year of our reign.

Kidd's Admission of Buried Treasure Ignored

After receiving the death penalty, Captain Kidd wrote the following letter to Robert Harley, Speaker of the House of Commons from Newgate Prison offering to lead the government's representative to treasure he had buried in the "Indies." However, the Speaker ignored the letter considering it a desperate attempt to save his neck from the gallows and the letter of the law.

S'r,
The sence of my present Condition (being under Condemnation) and the thoughts of having bene imposed on by such as seek't my destruction thereby to fulfill their ambitious desires makes me uncapable of Expressing my selfe in those terms as I ought, therefore due most humbly pray that you will be pleased to represent to the Hon'bl. house of Comons that in my late proceedings in the Indies I have lodged goods and Tresure to the value of one hundred thousand pounds, which I desire the Government may have the benefitt of, in order thereto, I shall desire no manner of liberty but to be kept prisoner on board such shipp as may be appointed for that purpose, and only give the necessary directions and in case I faile therin I desire no favour but to be forthwith Executed acording to my Sentence. If y'r honbl. house will please to order a Comittee to come to me, I doubt not but to give such satisfaction as may obtaine mercy, most Humbly submitting to the wisdom of your great assembly I am

S'r Y'r Unfortunate humble servant

(The actual signature of Wm Kidd on the last letter he would ever write)

Capt Kidd Treasure Maps

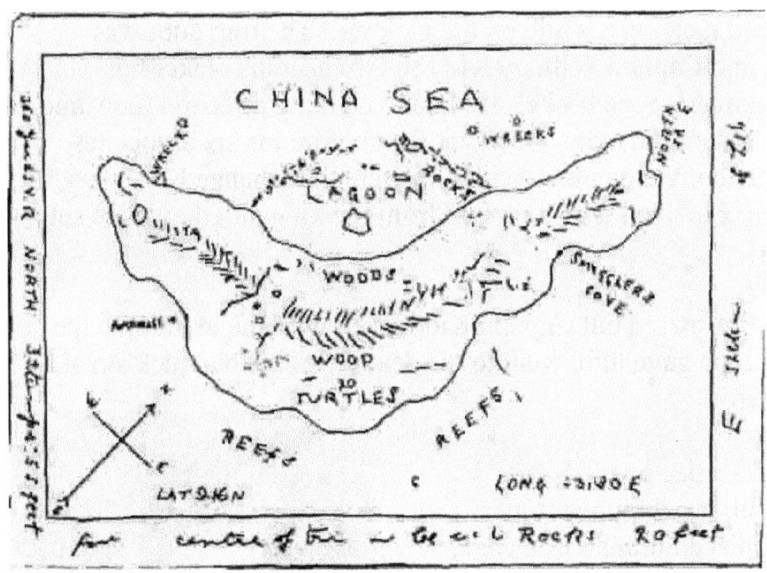

Found in what is believed to be Captain Kidd's sea chest in England

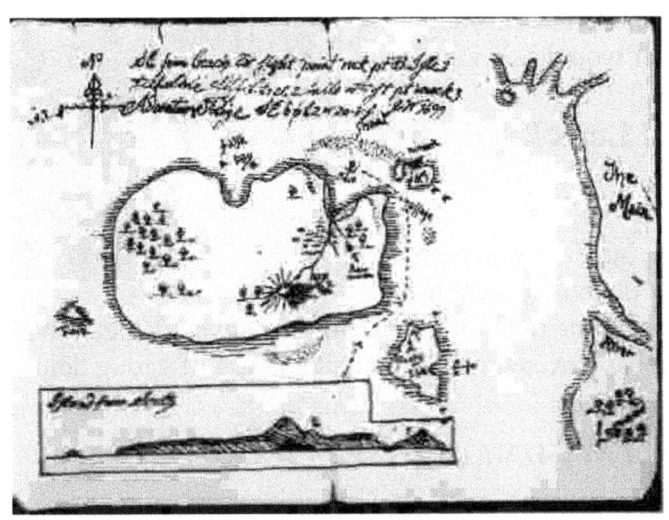

Kidd's Treasure Map found in
New England by the late Edward Rowe Snow

Bad Luck Streak Continues

More bad luck even while on the gallows. The trap door was sprung and Captain William Kidd fell to meet his maker but ... the hangman's rope broke! He had to be hung a second time, and this time the rope held. However, just before his six associates that were convicted along with him were to be hanged, a messenger arrived with a pardon from the king and they were set free.

They were spared but Captain Kidd, even with the extra time the broken rope gave him, went to his death with his bad luck streak unbroken.

The authorities painted Kidd's body with tar, wrapped it in chains, placed it in an iron cage, and hung him overlooking the Thames River, London. For nearly two years his body remained gibbeted as an example to deter other would-be-pirates.

More Bad Luck Even After his Death

Nearly three hundred years after his hanging, documents that had been misfiled at the time of his trial were uncovered and, if available then, would have exonerated him of all charges of wrong doing.

CAPTAIN KIDD NEVER WAS A PIRATE!

Three hundred years after his death, Captain William Kidd was proven innocent of all charges.

"Black" Sam Bellamy (1689 – 1717)

Shipwrecks, Witches, Treachery, Sunken Treasure and, Ghosts

Painting by Don Maitz

Samuel Bellamy was born in Devonshire, England in 1689. In the early 1700s, as a young teen, he left England to seek his fortune in the West Indies where he joined Captain Jennings and the British privateer fleet then at war against Spain. He was berthed aboard the sloop *Barsheba* and based at Port Royal in Jamaica.

Privateers were pirates by another name and were sponsored by their government. They were provided "Letters of Marque" which gave them the authorization to "pirate" ships free from fear of punishment in the event of their capture.

Sam Bellamy was a large black-haired man. He is reported to have been an intelligent and popular leader of men with a reputation for being generous to his victims. Some would later refer to him as the "Prince of Pirates".

It was probably during time spent in the Caribbean that he heard the stories of fantastic wealth lying on the bottom of the sea just waiting to be found. Tales of sunken Spanish treasure that would make a man richer than any king in Europe were standard seaman issue of the era.

It was here that he also was exposed to strategies and techniques he would later use during his short and very successful pirating career in the Caribbean.

He left his wife and child in Cantebury, England.. He would go back to the Caribbean, retrieve the legendary Spanish treasures and return a rich man.

His original plan was to locate and retrieve treasurer from a fleet of Spanish galleons that were known to have sunk off the Florida coast. For nearly one hundred years tales of a sunken Spanish galleon fleet laden with silver and gold had flamed the imagination of adventuresome young men in Europe. Perhaps the most famous of these stories was of Philip IV's treasure ship fleet heavily laden with riches that was destroyed in a great storm as it began its return to Spain.

King Philip IV depended upon the gold, silver, and copper treasures extracted from Spain's mines in the New World to fund his vast military establishment. However, the fleet of 1622 was delayed in sailing and left Havana at the height of the hurricane season. The entire fleet was lost when it sailed into the teeth of a violent hurricane. Remnants of this fleet are being found off Florida's coast even to this day. To provide a sense of scale to the enormity of this lost treasure, more than four tons of silver and gold have been reportedly retrieved from one wreck alone!

The thoughts of vast treasure apparently provided motive enough for Sam Bellamy to leave his wife and child half a world away. The lure of treasure allowed him to be successful in persuading a wealthy patron to finance a ship and crew to enable his adventure. After fitting out his newly acquired sloop with sufficient provisions and gear, he and his crew set of for the New World early in 1716.

According to folklore he came ashore at Eastham Harbor Cape Cod apparently to find rest and provisions before his continued trip south to Florida.

The Saga of Maria "Goody" Hallett – *Bellamy's Paramour*

It was here that young Sam Bellamy met and seduced the very beautiful Eastham farm girl, Maria Hallett, in the spring of 1716. Maria was a naïve fifteen year old farm girl from a well respected, church going Eastham family

The handsome sailor's sweet talk and tales of treasure and adventure impressed the wide-eyed Maria. He convinced her that he would marry her when he returned laden with silver, gold and jewels that he would recover from sunken treasure ships in the Caribbean. As Fall approached and the days shortened and grew cooler, he sailed south to begin his great adventure.

Goody Hallett

That Winter Maria was found lying in a cold Eastham barn with her dead baby in her arms. She was at once taken into town and attached to deacon Doane's whipping post and given several lashes before being thrown into jail. The selectmen spoke of charging her with murder. They said she must be made an example to others of the godless younger generation of the day.

It seemed that no cell could contain the young lass, and she continually escaped to wander the shore calling out the name of her lost love. Eastham gave up its attempts to keep her in jail and released the young girl upon the condition she would leave town and never return.

She made her home in a shack near the shore at South Wellfleet and eked out a living by doing menial jobs. In short order, the once most beautiful girl in Eastham had become haggard and worn and unrecognizable to those who had known her before Bellamy.

His Lover Labeled a Witch

Townspeople were convinced that she was a witch, and they now referred to as "Goody" Hallett. The name Goody, as defined in the American College Dictionary, was "a polite term applied to a woman in humble life."

Goody must have been extremely depressed and traumatized experiencing the death of her baby. Then to be shunned by friends and family, jailed then driven out of town combined perhaps causing her to lose her mind.

All of this happened in the era of the famous Salem witch trials so it was in keeping with the times for the town folks to condemn her as a witch, a person who had sold her soul to the devil. Goody would continually be seen walking the high Wellfleet cliffs gazing out to sea screaming curses into the winds on even the stormiest of Winter nights. Even today her ghost is said to walk the seaside cliffs of Cape Cod's outer shore near where Captain Black's ship went down in 1717.

Witch on the Dunes

Could witch Goody have had a hand in brewing storms that shipwrecked more than two thousand ships and drowned uncounted thousands of mariners, including her lover captain Black Bellamy, on the sandbars off South Wellfleet? There are those who believe she did.

On that fateful day in April 1717, at the height of the fierce storm, she was seen on the beach as the Whydah was sinking and sailors were drowning in the raging surf. People on the beach say they saw her high on the cliff shrieking thanks to the Devil for vengeance. All this happened off the South Wellfleet dunes near the lonely dilapidated shack in which Goody lived.

Goody Swallowed by a Whale?

Lynne McIlveen Illustration

"On April 22, 1751, she succumbed to the sea and was demolished by one of the whales off the coast. Further proof of this lies in the fact that when one of the whales was captured and cut open, inside they found Maria's red slippers."

Other tales have Goody riding upon the backs of whales with lanterns affixed to their tails in order to lure unsuspecting mariners onto the reefs and shoals of the outer cape referred to at the time as the "Graveyard of the Atlantic".

She is also supposed to have the power, as she was a witch, to conjure up storms and gales to the peril of seamen of the day. Some say it was she that brewed the storm that sank the Whydah and sent her scallywag lover to Davy Jones' locker.

Goody Hallett

Words and Music by Kiya Heartwood

Available for purchase at
www.wishingchair.com/music-group-7.html

They took the last man from the sea
But I swore I would never go
I knew she'd taken my love from me
Taken him down below

The first time I saw his raven hair
It was tied with a small dark bow
Four pistols he wore in his velvet coat
I never saw a man so bold

He said my name is Samuel Bellamy
Prince of all I obtain
Then he leaned and whispered in my ear
Girl tell me your name

We tarried in the Wellfleet shops
And down in Eastham town
Then he asked my father if I could wed
But my father turned him down

Say's there's talk you left
A wife and babe
Back in Cheltenham
But Sam he stared him in the eyes
He said, I'll take her and I can

Then Sam and Palgrave Williams heard
Of galleons from Spain
Laden with gold and indigo
Lost in a hurricane

So Sam set his mind on treasure to
Salvage from the sea

He said, I'll go and find the tallest ship
And I'll bring it back for thee

We said goodbye along the cliffs
And we made love fierce and wild
Then he took our plans
He took my soul
And he left me with his child.

Yes a boy was born
But soon he died
And they put me in their jail
They called me witch
And they called me whore
But I kept watch for his sails.

It was early that April morn
The sky was red and grey
But black that day soon became
That stole my love away

Yes her mast was cracked
Her hull was split
But I could hear the Whydah's bell
And she rang out the last
Sounds of hope
My true loves farewell

Now I walk the cliffs
And curse the sea
And every wind that blows
For the happiness we almost had
Now I will never know

The Beginning of Bellamy's Pirating Career

By all accounts Sam Bellamy was a rouge and a simple, blustering windbag of a man. His adventuresome spirit and gift of gab had enabled him to finance his quest for gold and also to seduce the loveliest girl on Cape Cod, Goody Hallett.

From the Cape, Bellamy sailed to Newport, RI where he met Paulsgrave Williams. Paulsgrave came from a successful family. Bellamy was apparently successful in infecting Williams with gold fever and convinced Williams to contribute funds for his Caribbean adventure. The pair left Rhode Island together to begin their hunt for sunken Spanish treasure.

They searched for several months but, try as they would, had no luck finding any trace of sunken Spanish treasure as originally planned. Not wanting to return home as failures, together they decided that finding treasure on ships moving upon the surface of the water, rather than those sitting at the bottom of the sea, would be a much more profitable course of action. They would make their fortune as pirates.

The two men met the notorious pirate Benjamin Hornigold and decided to join his crew of cut throats. It would appear that Captain Hornigold ran sort of a pirate training school as it was upon his ship that the later infamous Blackbeard also first sailed the Caribbean as a novice pirate.

Captain Hornigold was born in England and accordingly would only attack French and Spanish ships, not English ships. In June 1716, his crew revolted against him because they wanted to attack an English ship.

The crew voted Samuel Bellamy and Paulsgrave Williams as the new Captain and Quartermaster, respectively.

Bellamy and his crew plundered more than fifty ships making him one of the most successful pirates in the Caribbean. He was now known as "Black Bellamy" or "Black Sam". Perhaps his nickname, "Black", was a reference to his preference for the expensive black clothes he always wore. Dressed all in black, and with four dueling pistols around his waist, he was a formidable figure.

Black Sam was a fine strategist. He would employ two ships in his raids. The first, his flagship, was armed with many cannons but relatively slow. The second, captained by Paulsgrave Williams, was lightly armed but fast. With this combination of assets Black Sam was able to coordinated attacks and capture ships with relative ease without damaging them.

With his ship loaded with this treasure and the booty plundered from more than fifty other ships, Black Bellamy and his crew decided to retire from pirating. They were now richer than their wildest imaginations could ever have imagined.

Whydah in a Storm

Black Sam and his crew set a Northerly course and headed for home. For some home was in New England; for others, home was further away in England. Where was Black Sam heading? Was he going home to the wife and child left in England, or was he returning, as promised, to the young farm girl he seduced on Cape Cod?

Some, who believe he was returning for the Cape's Goody Hallett, will refer to Black Sam Bellamy as the "Romantic Pirate." If returning to Goody was his plan, perhaps those in England would call him a different name.

On April 26, near Cape Cod, Whydah and its crew of 148 souls ran into an intense late Winter storm. Despite

Herculean efforts of the crew, the Whydah struck the bar off South Wellfleet near what is now Marconi Beach in the Cape Cod National Seashore Park and sank as raging surf tore her to pieces.

Wellfleet near what is now Marconi Beach in the Cape Cod National Seashore Park and sank as a raging surf tore her to pieces.

People along the beach watching the tragic scene reported hearing and seeing "Goody" Hallett high upon the dunes screaming thanks to the Devil for vengeance.

The next day a search for survivors and perhaps treasure revealed only bits and pieces of floating remains of the once proud flagship Whydah and her crew.

Paulgrave's ship, the "Mary Anne," had stopped at Block Island in Rhode Island so he could visit his mother and thereby avoided the storm.

Only two survived the Wydah's sinking and live to tell the stories of Captain Black Sam Bellamy: an Indian pilot and Thomas Davis, a Welsh carpenter. Nothing is known of what became of the pilot, but it was Davis' vivid account of the shipwreck that was passed from generation to generation to become part of Cape Cod folklore. Essentially all that is known of Black Sam the pirate comes from stories recounted by Thomas Davis. Thomas Davis was jailed, tried, and acquitted of piracy.

"The Encyclopedia Americana" says of Samuel Bellamy, "...a notorious pirate, was wrecked in his ship, the Whidah, of 23 guns and 130 men, off Wellfleet, on Cape Cod, in April 1717, after having captured several vessels on the coast and an indecisive engagement with a French ship proceeding to Quebec.

Only one Indian and one Englishman escaped of his crew. Six of the pirates, who had been run ashore when drunk a few days previous, by the captain of the captured vessel, were hung in Boston in November 1717. "Black Sam," as he was known by then, was never seen again, nor was his body ever recovered."

Legend of "Goody's" Buried Treasure

Some legends say that "Goody" had retrieved a chest of pirate gold from the surf that stormy night and buried it somewhere in the Wellfleet dunes. Because "Goody" Hallett had "lost her mind" she apparently forgot where she buried the treasure for she continued to eek out a meager living until the day she died. If she did bury treasure, she kept the whereabouts a secret and took the location with her to her grave.

Another story of buried treasure has the two survivors Thomas Davis and John Julian visiting the house of Samuel Hardings in Wellfleet on the night of the disaster. According to the story…the next morning, the three men hitched up Hardings' wagon and retrieved several wagonloads of the wreck's treasure from the beach. They secreted it in Hardings' barn before hiding it more securely, perhaps by burying the fortune somewhere on the Harding property.

Treasure being buried in the dunes

About a week after the wreck, Governor Shute sent a Captain Cypian Southack to the Cape to recover as much of the pirate treasure as possible. He searched some private homes and commandeered some of the salvaged good but found no trace of the cargo.

Is there still buried gold somewhere in the Wellfleet dunes? Perhaps the treasure still lies beneath the sand where Goody buried it waiting to be uncovered or has it already been found?

It is rumored that Sam Bellamy's ghost still walks Wellfleet's cliffs and dunes in search of his lost treasure. To this day gold coins can be found on Wellfleet's beach after big storms.

Was Captain Black Bellamy Tricked into Eternity?

In the spring of 1717, Bellamy and Williams are reported to have captured seven ships on their return trip to Cape Cod. Approaching the Cape, Consort Captain Williams, aboard sloop Mary Anne, stopped at Block Island, an island just south of Cape Cod, to visit family

The weather was deteriorating as the rest of Bellamy's fleet continued north to the Cape. One of the ships was a wine carrying sloop captained by a native Cape Codder. Legend has Bellamy promising this captain the return of his ship if he would lead the fleet into the safe harbor at Provincetown.

 He was made this remarkable promise because he had extensive knowledge of the treacherous, shoaled waters off the Outer Cape known as the graveyard of the North Atlantic. The bones of literally thousands of hapless ships lay upon its sandy ocean bottom.

A lantern was hung in the rigging so that Bellamy and his flagship the Whydah would be able to follow in the darkness of the moonless night.

The wily Cape Cod captain apparently had other plans. He allowed the pirates left onboard to guard the prize to become drunk on the cargo of wine the ship carried. Then, with his captors thus incapacitated, he tossed a burning tar barrel overboard for the Whydah to follow into eternity via the sandy treacherous sandy shoals of the Outer Cape while he sailed safely into Provincetown harbor. Some of the pirates were caught in Provincetown, put on trial and hanged in Boston. Thoreau mentions the Whydah tragedy in his book, *Cape Cod*. He wrote,``A storm coming on, their whole fleet was wrecked, and more than a hundred dead bodies lay along the shore." The shore he references is Marconi Beach in Wellfleet.

Whydah Discovered off Wellfleet

In 1984 the wreck of the "Whydah" was discovered by Barry Clifford of Tisbury, Massachusetts in the shallow waters off of Wellfleet. The value of the treasure is estimated by some to approximate $400 million dollars.

I'm from the Government and I'm Here to Help

News of shipwrecked treasure traveled very fast. Within days officials in Boston sent a ship to the Cape to "protect the government's interests." In other words, confiscate the treasure. Posters were immediately put up warning that anyone found with shipwreck goodswould face a severe penalty. The government's men scoured the beaches, searched barns, sheds, yards and houses for miles around attempting to uncover booty of any kind. They confiscated several wagonloads of goods but no serious treasure was uncovered.

Prior to the arrival of the government ship, hundreds of men from all across the Cape had scoured the beach of anything of value. Reportedly the only thing left for the government team to recover was the pirate ship's anchor cable.

Centuries later the state of Massachusetts would claim joint ownership of the *Whydah* and demand to regulate the salvage of any artifacts and treasure it might contain. The difference this time was that lawyers were dispatched to confiscate treasure and not a ship. After several years the suit was settled in favor of the treasure hunter Barry Clifford, the man who had invested fifteen years and countless dollars in order to find the treasure ship.

George and Rachel Wall,

Boston's husband and wife pirate team

She was the last woman to be hanged in Boston.

B 175? – d 1789 She was born Rachel Schmidt on a farm outside of Carlisle, PA some- time in the late 1750s.

She eloped with and married George Wall when she was about sixteen and they moved to Boston where she was a chamber-maid on Beacon Hill and he a fisherman. George signed aboard a privateer during the American Revolution and was there exposed to the life of a privateer, which is essentially a pirate with a Letter of Marque.

After four years as a privateer George and a few compatriots stole a sloop in Essex, MA.

They established a base of operation pretending to be a family of fishermen, first on Appledore Island and then later the Isles of Shoals off the Maine, New Hampshire coast.

They concocted a very devious plan that proved equally effective and ruthless. They would set their small sloop adrift in the path of ship traffic with George and the other men hiding below decks leaving young Rachael alone topside. When a passing ship came within earshot Rachael would begin her 'Damsel in Distress" act by running up the distress flag and screaming for help at the top of her lungs.

Captain Sandy Gordon

How his Pirate Career Began

Sandy Gordon was a crewman aboard one Captain John Herring's British ship PORPOISE. In the summer of 1714 Captain Herring had his teenage daughter aboard the PORPOISE. Sandy Gordon was discovered by the Captain in an uncompromising position with young Martha, in her cabin.

The captain ordered 72 lashes of the whip, which almost killed him, as punishment. After his wounds had healed, Sandy sought revenge, and persuaded much of the PORPOISE crew to mutiny.

Seizing the ship, Sandy and ten men killed all crewmen who remained loyal to the Captain, then he strapped Martha's father to the mast and gave him 72 lashes of the whip every hour until he was dead.

Gordon began his pirate career by taking three English merchant vessels off the coast of Scotland. However, because Captain Sandy Gordon refused to share the little treasure they confiscated from these vessels with his mutinous crew they mutinied against him. They put him ashore on an island off Scotland with Martha Herring.

Living in a fisherman's shanty for many months, Sandy and Martha were visited by pirates who had come ashore for water. Blackbeard. Blackbeard apparently got a kick out of Sandy's plight of being marooned by the PORPOISE crew, so he allowed Sandy to join him.

Sailing the Atlantic, the pirate fleet captured a French brig and a Spanish galleon containing over $1,000,000 in gold and silver, on its way to the King of Spain. The French brig was renamed the FLYING SCOT by Blackbeard, and given to Sandy Gordon to command, as a reward for his bravado in the fight with the French and Spaniards.

The pirate vessels were now so filled with treasure that Blackbeard decided to head for the nearest landfall to rid themselves of some of it — the nearest landfall, a port where pirates were welcomed, was New Hampshire's Isles of Shoals. Here Sandy Gordon married Martha Herring and settled at White Island, one of the Isles, but their honeymoon was brief.

The English Navy had been searching the Atlantic for the mutineers for over a year. A man-of-war came to the Isles shortly after Sandy and Martha set up housekeeping on White Island.

Gordon went out to battle the naval warship. Two well-directed broadsides by the British man-of-war sank the FLYING SCOT like a rock, with Sandy Gordon, in his favorite bright red uniform, going down with her. Reportedly, only two of the pirate crew survived the sinking, and they were picked up by the British crew and hanged at the yardarm that very day.

The only member of the pirate band left at the Isles was Martha Herring Gordon, who died there in 1735.

Celia Thaxter writes, *"Teach's comrade, Captain Scott(Gordonj brought this lovely lady hither. They buried immense treasure on the islands; that of Scott(Gordon) was buried on an island apart from the rest...The maiden was carried to the island where her pirate lover's treasure was hidden, and made to swear with horrible rites, that until his return, if it were not till the day of judgement, she would guard it from search of all mortals. So, there she paces still...She laments like a Banshee before the tempest, wailing through the gorges at Appledore."*

Blackbeard the Pirate

Edward Teach a/k/a Blackbeard b 1680 – d 1718 was an English sailor whose piracy career began in 1716 and ended on November 22, 1718 in a bloody battle off Ocracoke Inlet, North Carolina.

He terrorized shipping from the Caribbean to New England at the height of the period known as the "Golden Age of Piracy."

Before turning to piracy, Teach had gallantly served England as a privateer in the "Queen Anne's War that ended in 1713.

He learned the tricks of the pirate's trade from pirate Benjamin Hornigold.

Hornigold rewarded Teach by gifting him with a ship they had hijacked. Teach renamed this craft "Queen Anne's Revenge" and outfitted her with 40 cannon and a crew of 300 and was off to pirate on his own. He cruised the Caribbean and the coastal waters of the American colonies as far north as Maine in New England attacking shipping, stealing cargos, torturing passengers and crews and leaving havoc in his wake.

Having a fearful persona and a reputation of being heartless was as important to the success of a pirate as were the number of cannons aboard his fleet. Pirates used symbolism along with their actions to instill terror into the hearts of all whom they approached.

Not all pirate flags were skulls and cross bones as Blackbeard's flag or "Jolly Roger" illustrates

Blackbeard's flag depicting a heart dripping blood while a devil skeleton held an hourglass and spear, was designed to strike fear in his victims. It apparently worked as many captains reportedly gave up their ships without firing a shot when they spied the "Jolly Roger."

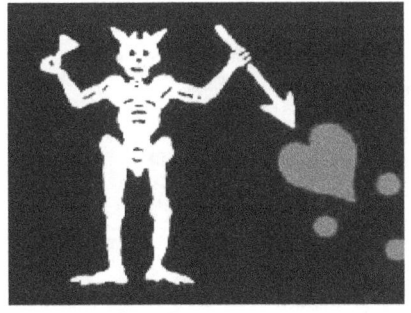

Blackbeard was a very large man with long, thick black hair and beard and wore a constant scowl upon his face. His natural wild eyed appearance was indeed frightening. To heighten his fearsome appearance Blackbeard would go into battle with lighted hemp tapers in his beard and hair. He was a frightening sight indeed and, to many, appeared to be some kind of supernatural devil.

Blackbeard would arm himself with an arsenal of weapons in preparation for battle. He would carry several loaded pistols on cords around his neck and a few more in his

bandolier. The multiple pistols were an advantage when attacking as pistols of the day were single shot weapons. In addition to carrying multiple pistols he also would arm himself with several swords, daggers and knives.

His fearsome image and reputation, which he cultivated, has carried over to this day as the name Blackbeard still conjures up visions of a ruthless pirate.

Blackbeard's buried treasure in New England

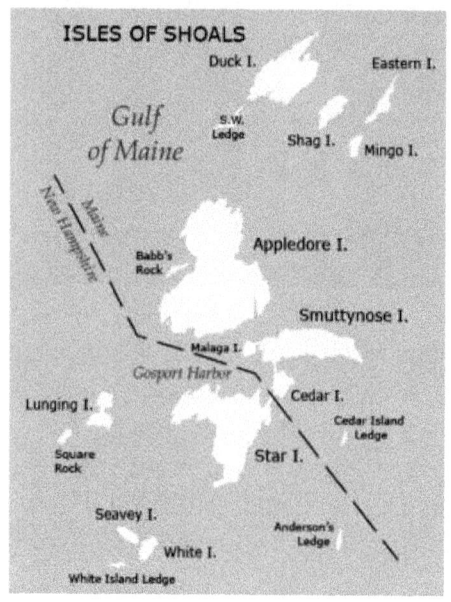

The Isles of Shoals are a group of nine islands located six miles off the coast of Maine and New Hampshire. These islands lie right in the path of shipping coming from and going to Europe following the warm currents of the Gulf Stream.

Malaga (ME), the smallest of the islands being only 300 by 500 feet, is said to have been named by Spanish mariners early in the Sixteenth century.

In the 1820s four bars of silver found on the island by captain Samuel Haley were sold by him to fund the construction of a breakwater to connect Malaga with the larger Smuttynose island.

Smuttynose (ME) is also where the Spanish bark "Sagunto" sank on January, 14 1813. All hands on board died. Fourteen were found over the next few days, some having crawled ashore only to meet their maker as a frozen corpse. No treasure or cargo has ever been reported recovered.

Blackbeard took fourteen wives and fathered forty children. He is said to have honeymooned on Smuttynose with his thirteenth before leaving her to guard the treasure while awaiting his return. One legend reports that Blackbeard buried treasure on a halfmoon shaped beach somewhere on Smuttynose Island.

He never did return and his bride's ghost is still occasionally seen on the island. Is she still guarding the location of the treasure or is her spirit awaiting the return of her black hearted lover?

Lunging island (NH) is the location most strongly rumored to still hold Blackbeard's buried treasure. The treasure is said to be secreted in a cave long since collapsed and covered by nearly 300 years of storm and tide.

The end of a career

Blackbeard bid his newest wife and treasure farewell and sailed south to his favorite hunting grounds off the Carolinas. It was here he was to marry his fourteenth wife, Mary Ormond of Bath, North Carolina and meet his maker in waters near Ocracoke Village, North Carolina.

Blackbeard found the inland and coastal waterways ideal conditions within which he would conduct his trade. The confined waterway, with its shallow coves and inlets, were ideal for hunting commercial ships and avoiding capture by larger deep drafted naval vessels. Life was good here for the pirates. Not only were physical conditions conducive to pirating but, in addition, Blackbeard had bribed the colonial governor, Charles Eden, to leave them alone in return for a share of the booty.

At one point Blackbeard had several ships in his pirate fleet and commanded more than seven hundred men. He terrorized the Carolina coast for eighteen months including a blockade of Charleston.

His career would come to an end when irate Carolinians appealed in desperation to the then governor of Virginia, Governor Spotswood, for aid. Spotswood engaged Royal Navy Lieutenant Robert Maynard to assemble a task force and put an end to Blackbeard's reign of terror.

On November 22, 1718, Maynard's two shallow drafted sloops *Ranger* and *Jane* with sixty-two men found Blackbeard anchored in Ocracoke Inlet preparing his newest ship *Adventurer* for battle.

Although outmanned by almost four to one Blackbeard came close to winning the battle. However, Blackbeard was fooled into leading a charge aboard Maynard's vessel as Maynard had hidden his main force below decks thereby luring Blackbeard's lesser numbers into a trap. Maynard and his men emerged and proceeded to cut down the outnumbered pirates one by one.

Blackbeard in battle

The fight ended when Teach fell. He was shot five times and stabbed more than twenty and finnaly stopped fighting when he finally was decapitated. His body thrown overboard and legend holds the body swam around the ship seven times before finally sinking in the channel that now bears his name, Teach's Hole.

Teach's head was placed as a trophy on the bowsprit of Maynard's ship. In order to claim his reward Maynard was required to submit Blackbeard's head to governor Spotswood as proof. Later, the head was hung from a pike in Bath, North Carolina where it stayed for many years.

Blackbeard was very proficient at self promotion. He wanted his persona and reputation strike fear into all. As example, one legend reports Blackbeard as blustering that he shot his own first mate, because "if he didn't shoot one or two [crewmen] now and then, they'd forget who he was." His self promotion was more successful than he could have ever imagined. Three hundred years later his reputation and giant sized legend continues larger than ever with scores of books, movies, television programs produced memorializing him for the ages.

Quarter - deriving from the idea of "shelter", quarter was given when the sailors offered mercy. To give no quarter was to indicate that none would be spared. Quarter was often the prize given to a honourable loser in a sailor fight. If enraged, however, a sailor would deprive the loser any such luxury.

Pirate Captain Jack Quelch

In July, 1703, John Quelch was a lieutenant on the "Charles," a ship based in Marblehead, Massachusetts. The *Charles's* crew mutinied and locked the ailing Captain Plowman in his cabin. The crew elected Quelch the captain and Plowman was thrown overboard

Under Quelch'a command the crew plundered nine Portuguese ships off the coast of Brazil. The total value is estimated at over 4 million in today's money.

"Old Roger"

Quelch was captured north of Cape Cod while hiding gold nuggets on Smuttynose Island. Also, before their capture, legend says the crew buried some of the gold on Star Island across from Smuttynose Island. In the 1800s some gold coins were found hidden in a stone wall there. No one has reported finding more coins. Does that mean no more has been found and that all the gold is gone?

Old Roger

Popular myth has it that John Quelch flew a pirate flag referred to as Old Roger by his crew. It is sometimes considered to be the origin of the name Jolly Roger. It is alleged that his theme was later borrowed by Blackbeard and also Bartholomew "Black Bart" Roberts.

There is no evidence whatsoever that Quelch flew any flag other than the Flag of St. George or possibly a privateer's flag of St. George quartered on a red background similar to today's British merchant colors.

Courtroom testimony from the crew maintained that the flag of England had been flown at all times.

Captain Ned (Edward) LOWE

Cruelest pirate upon the seas

Born in London, England in the late 1700s, he was a petty thief and pickpocket before coming to Boston where he became legitimately employed as rigger in one of Boston's many shipyards.

In May 1722 he and group of others set sail for Honduras.

The original plan was to steal a shipload of lumber for resale in Boston. Something went wrong and he and his crew were forced off the ship. The next day Lowe, and his soon to be pirates, stole a sloop and set of in search of ships to plunder. After capturing several ships he chose the 80 ton schooner *The Fancy* as flagship of his pirate fleet.

Stamp commemorating Ned Lowe

Lowe was described as a "maniac and a brute" by his own crew. His needless brutality was so severe that authorities made particular efforts to capture him and eventually his crew cast him adrift mid ocean in a small boat without any provisions.

Some examples of his senseless cruel and brutal actions, He;

- Made the commander of a Nantucket whaler slice off his own ears and eat them before he killed him,
- Personally slaughtered fifty-three officers of the Spanish galleon "Montcova", and forced one, before killing him, to eat the heart of a fellow officer.
- Cut off a victim's lips, cooked them, and forced the victim to eat his own lips before he slaughtered him,
- Burned a French cook alive saying he was a "greasy fellow who would fry well"

- Lowe is said to have enjoyed torturing his captives. Few who were taken as captives aboard Low's ship ever debarked alive.

- One of his sadistic torture sessions apparently went wrong and Lowe was cut severely about his mouth. The medical attention he received went wrong and he was left with an ugly scar as his reward.

- He was the captain who the real Robinson Crusoe, Marblehead's Philip Ashton, escaped from by hiding on a deserted Caribbean island in June of 1722.

- Lowe's end came after he was rescued from the sea, having been set adrift by his own crew, by a passing French ship. However, when they discovered his true identity, the French mariners gave him a cursory trial and then hung him from the yardarm until he was dead. The year was 1724.

- Another version of Low's demise has the sadistic pirate aboard the *Fancy* off the Canary Islands where he is reported to have drowned when his ship sank in a violent storm with the loss of all hands.

Philip Ashton - b 1702 – d ?

The real Robinson Crusoe hailed from Marblehead captured by Pirate Edward Lowe

Born in Marblehead, Massachusetts he was the real life Robinson Crusoe who spent sixteen months as a castaway on Roatan Island in the Bay of Honduras in 1723/24. The book Robinson Crusoe, published in 1725 are said to be based upon Philip Ashton.

"Robinson Crusoe"

Philip was a fisherman who, while fishing off of the coast of Nova Scotia in June of 1723, was captured by the infamous Pirate Edward Lowe.

Ten months later he managed to escape his captors by hiding in the jungle when they landed on a small deserted island to take on fresh water. He was free from the grasp of his captors but had only the rags upon his back. Lacking tools, knife or weapons of any kind he could not hunt for game so he lived on fruits and berries.

Later he met an Englishman who mysteriously appeared out of the jungle, stayed a short while then dissapeared back into the jungle leaving behind a few tools, gun and gunpowder, tobacco and other supplies. His diet became more varied as he would now hunt game and make fire to cook a hot meal.

Ashton was finally rescued by the ship Diamond that hailed from Salem, Mass returning him safely home, May, 1st 1726 being gone nearly three years after his captured by pirates.

Pirate Captain William Fly

Should he have been called "Black Fly"?

Captain William Fly (died July 12, 1726) was an English pirate who raided New England shipping until he was captured by the crew of a seized ship. He was hanged in Boston, Massachusetts.

William Fly's career as a pirate began in April 1726 when he signed on to sail with Captain John Green to West Africa on the *Elizabeth*. Green and Fly began to clash until one night William led a mutiny that resulted in Capt. Green being tossed overboard; Fly then took command of the *Elizabeth*. Having captured the ship, the mutineers sewed a Jolly Roger flag, renamed the ship *Fames' Revenge*, elected William Fly as captain, and sailed to the coast of North Carolina and north toward New England.

Gibbeted Pirate

They captured five ships in about two months before being captured themselves. Following his capture, Cotton Mather tried, and failed, to get Fly to publicly repent. William Fly and his crew were hanged at Boston Harbor on July 12, 1726. Reportedly, Fly approached the hanging with complete disdain and even reproached the hangman for doing a poor job, re-tying the noose and placing it about his neck with his own two hands. His last words were, roughly, a warning to captains to treat their sailors well and pay them on time. Following the hanging, his body was hung in chains (gibbeted) on Nixes Mate Island in Boston Harbor, to serve as a warning to other sailors not to turn to piracy.

1726 Newspaper account of William Fly's short career as a pirate and his capture

Dated August 18. 1726

hurt.

Boston, July 4. The Elizabeth Snow of Bristol, John Green Commander, sailing from Jamaica the latter End of April, or Beginning of May last, bound for Guinea, kept Company with the Fleet till he got through the Gulf of Florida. He lost the Fleet one Morning, and the Night following his People on board, being Eleven in Number, all (except the Doctor, Carpenter, and Gunner) mutiny'd, and murder'd the Captain, and Chief Mate, and cast them overboard on the 27th of May last. They then proceeded for the Coast of New England in a Pyratical Manner, taking several Vessels, among which was a Snow from North Carolina, bound to this Place, taken by them the 3d of June, on board of which Sloop was one William Atkinson a Passenger, who was detain'd by them to navigate their Snow (they not having any Navigator on board.) After which they took a Scooner belonging to Marblehead; and having put on board of it seven of their Gang, they left the Snow, commanded by Captain Fly, (who was Captain Green's Boatswain when murder'd) he having then but three reputed Pyrates with him, the rest being forced Men. On the 23d of June, Atkinson taking this Advantage, with the Assistance of three more forced Men, surprized and secured Fly and his three Accomplices, and brought the Snow and them, and deliver'd them up to the Government here on Wednesday last. The Men are now secured in Jail, in order to be try'd this day by a Court of Admiralty.

Palgrave Williams

Rhode Island's Royal Pirate

Palgrave Williams served as Black Sam Bellamy's quartermaster, then became captain of the sloop *Mary Anne*, in Bellamy's small fleet of pirate raiders.

Born in Rhode Island, the 39 year old Williams was a successful and very wealthy goldsmith from a prestigious family. When he met Samuel Bellamy in the fall of 1715, Sam apparently infected him with "Treasure Fever." Soon after their meeting the pair headed off to the Caribbean to retrieve sunken Spanish treasure.

Palgrave Williams in Battle

Search as they might they were unable to discover any sunken Spanish treasure so, rather than return home empty handed, they turned to piracy. In just a year of raiding Williams and Bellamy plundered more than 50 ships on the Caribbean and Atlantic.

He like Bellamy left his wife and children to begin a great treasure hunting adventure. Why would a very rich family man give it all up to fund a complete stranger on chance that treasure ships wrecked 100 years earlier could be found? Perhaps he suffered from a seventeenth century form of mid-life crisis.

Royal Roots and American Presidents

Williams could trace his roots to one of England's great families, the Mowbrays, who in the Middle Ages lived on the Isle of Axholme, Lincolnshire. It is through this family that British leaders, American Presidents, Hollywood stars, the present Queen of England and, Diana, Princess of Wales can claim to have a pirate on their family tree.

Williams is reportedly related to: Anne Boleyn, Elizabeth I, Sir Winston Churchill, Audrey Hepburn, George Washington, Thomas Jefferson and George W. Bush, two wives of Henry VIII, Pocahontas and the Duchess from *Alice in Wonderland*.

First a Quartermaster

Palgrave was elected quartermaster by the crew, as was the custom of the day. The quartermaster's job was to protect the crew's interests, and to act as a check-and-balance on the power of the captain. Next to the captain, he was the most important person aboard a pirate ship.

It is the duty of a quartermaster to run the day to day operations of the ship, sort of a COO of the sea. It is his responsibility to:

- manage ship's bookwork (therefore must be literate)
- assign work details,
- settle quarrels,
- maintain battle readiness,
- punish minor infractions,
- apportion provisions,
- assign battle stations,
- ensure booty is shared appropriately

A person elected to this position was respected by the pirates as a trustworthy, intelligent and responsible man. It was not unusual for a quartermaster to next be elected captain by the crew.

Then Bellamy's Consort Captain,

His first command was as Consort Captain of the sloop *Mary Anne*. A Consort Captain is a commander who commands a vessel accompanying another, such as Black Sam's flagship the Whydah.

Captains Bellamy and Williams would co-ordinate their attacks upon their prey with the agile *Mary Anne* cornering the prey and Black Sam's larger ship, bristling with scores of cannon, would intimidate essentially all their conquests into surrendering without a fight.

Ship similar to the Mary Anne

When the fleet sailed north from the Bahamas in the spring of 1717, Williams would take a detour that saved his life. He debarked at Block Island, Rhode Island, to visit his mother and sisters there and planned to rejoin the *Whydah* later. The *Mary Anne* would soon be shipwrecked, along with the *Whydah*, off the coast of Cape Cod

Williams would retire from piracy for a short time but, longing for the exciting life of a pirate, he went back to sea within a year. He would continue to plunder and raid innocent merchant ships for several more years. Then in 1723, at the age of 45, he retired a second and final time. Williams is said to have settled down with a new wife and name and began a second family. Unlike most pirates of the day, he escaped the gallows and died an uneventful death.

The Youngest Pirate
John King (b. 1706 or '07 – d. 1717)

The boy pirate, only nine years old when he joined Black Sam's crew

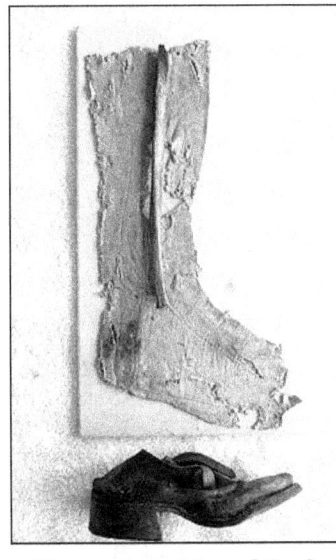

Shoe and stocking of the 9 year old pirate

Nine year old John King would not listen to his mother. She tried to warn him that becoming a pirate was not one of his better ideas. He and his mother were onboard the sloop "Bonetta" when the swashbuckling pirate, Black Sam Bellamy, captured the ship sailing from Antigua to Jamaica in November of 1716.

The pirates spent fifteen days transferring their plunder onto the Bonetta. In addition to taking anything of value the pirates took a Negro Man and an Indian Boy belonging to Mr. Benjamin Wicker.

During this period young John became enthralled with the wild excitement and daring that a pirate's life seemed it must be and he demanded he be allowed to go with the pirates or, he would kill himself. When his mother rejected his boyhood idea as folly he threatened to kill her as well, according to the deposition of the Bonetta's captain.

He further saith, that one John King who was coming as a passenger with him from the said Island of Jamaica to the Island of Antigua deserted his sloop, and went with the Pirates and was so far from being forced or compelled thereto by them as the deponent could perceive or learn that he declared he would Kill himself if he was Restrained, and even threatned his Mother who was then on Board as a Passenger with the Deponent.

The British Navy routinely would employ young boys as "powder monkeys" to move gunpowder from the ship's magazine to the cannons. However, no historical record exists suggesting a child so young as John King ever joined the British Navy or a band of pirates.

In 2006 divers found a bone, silk stocking, and shoe of what appeared to have belonged to a young boy of about a ten or 11 year old. Ancient Caribbean court records, documents in England and, twenty-first century forensic examinations combine to strongly suggest the bone is the remains of the youngest pirate ever identified, John King.

According to historian Ken Kinkor of the Expedition Whydah Sea-Lab & Learning Center in Provincetown, Massachussets, teen pirates were not uncommon during the early 18th century, "But this is the youngest one I have ever come across."

"The wreck was like a 300-year-old Wal-Mart on the bottom of the ocean with an unusually broad variety of artifacts stolen from other ships. Despite the quantity of materials recovered, we've never really discovered the mother lode of the ship" Ken said.

Richard Nolan

Consort captain

Consort Captain Nolan

He hailed from Dublin Ireland and served as quartermaster aboard Bellamy's Whydah and later he was made the "consort captain" of a ship in Bellamy's fleet.

A consort captain is essentially a sub-captain or one who serves under the "Fleet Commander," in this case, Black Sam Bellamy He apparently was not onboard the Whydah when she went down off Wellfleet but rather was aboard Williams' Mary Anne when it stopped at Block Island thereby avoiding a salty grave. He was with Williams as they pillaged the Maine coast awaiting Bellamy and the *Whydah*. They never came as they were on the bottom off a Cape Cod beach.

It is reported that he later sailed with the notorious Blackbeard, a fellow trainee aboard Hornigold's "pirate training" ship, for a while before he retired from piracy in 1718. After being pardon by the British crown he managed to become a respectable citizen. Later he would serve as a character witness at the trials of other pirates.

Swing the Lead - The Lead was a weight at the bottom of a line that gave sailors a way to measure depth when near land. To Swing the Lead was considered a simple job, and thusly came to represent one who is avoiding work or taking the easy work over the hard. In today's terms, one who swings the lead is a slacker

Hendrick Quintor

Fierce fighter

Quintor is thought to be the son of a seaman and his place of birth is uncertain. What is known is that he spent essentially all of his life at sea and was considered an extremely fierce fighter.

He was aboard a Spanish vessel in the Caribbean when it was captured by pirate captain Benjamin Hornigold. It was here that he met Black Sam Bellamy.

Later Hendrick would join others to depose captain Hendrick and elect Black Sam as captain. He would serve on the sloop Mary Anne, a ship in Bellamy's fleet.

Accordingly, Hendrick was not aboard when the Whydah went down in the storm off Cape Cod as the Mary Anne had stopped at Block Island and later was with Williams in Maine to pillage there awaiting the *Whydah*.

He and five others were soon captured, jailed in Boston, tried as pirates and found guilty of piracy. The penalty - death by hanging.

Keel Haul - This is the act of throwing a man overboard, tied to a rope that goes beneath the ship and then dragging him from one side to the other and hauling him out. Besides the torment of being dragged under water, this would drag the victim across the barnacle-studded ship's hull and cause great pain and injury. This was a serious punishment and not administered lightly.

Captain John Phillips

They pickled his head

Pickled head

John Phillips was an English shipwright aboard a vessel bound for Newfoundland when it was captured by the pirate ship *Good Fortune.*

Phillips decided to join the pirates and thus began a career that would end dramatically eight months laterDuring his seven and one half month career, Phillips and his band of cutthroats aboard "Revenge" reportedly captured thirty four ships in New England waters. His luck began to run out when, in March of 1724 off the shores of Cape Sable, when he was struck severely on the head by the captain of one of his prey. The wound, although severe, was not fatal and Phillips.

Later a ship from Cape Ann, Massachusetts overtook the "Revenge" and, after a bloody battle, Phillips and his men were captured. Phillips, by now quite weakened by the fierce fighting and his previous head wound, was forced to dance a jig for his captors until he dropped exhausted upon his own deck and died.

His captors cut off his head and pickled it so they could prove to officials in Boston that they had done in the infamous pirate Captain Phillips.

The survivors of his crew were tried and found guilty of murder and piracy and were all hanged June 2, 1724, on Bird Island, now part of Logan Airport, East Boston.

Tales of Where Pirates and Shipwreck Treasures May be Found

Isles of Shoals

Choice of Pirates for Centuries

The islands that comprise the Isle of Shoals: Star Island, Appledore Island, Smuttynose Island, White Island, Cedar Island, Duck Island, Lunging Island, Eastern Island, Shag Island, Mingo Island and Seavey Island, have been reported to have been favored by pirates since the 1600's.

Smuttynose Island, at 25 acres (10 ha), is the third-largest island. It is known as the site of Blackbeard's honeymoon, later for the shipwreck of the Spanish ship *Sagunto* in 1813,

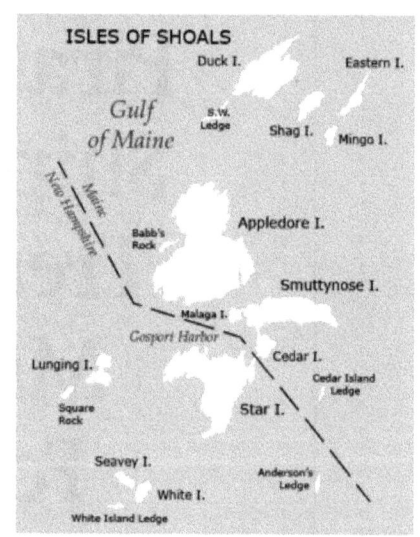

Malaga Island is a diminutive island just to the west of Smuttynose, connected to it by a breakwater. That breakwater was built around 1820 by Captain Samuel Haley, who is reputed to have paid for its construction with proceeds from four bars of pirate silver that he found under a flat rock on the island.

We have collected several legendary accounts of piratical activity in these islands. Many of the legends have been supported by the finds of gold and silver coins as well as silver bars.

How much treasure has been found and not reported will never be known.

We have compiled a collection of the island's legends of pirates and treasure

Spanish Galleon Runs Aground on Star Island

Some early records from Spain indicate that a Spanish galleon had crashed on the eastern shore of Star Island around 1685, at a spot known as Miss Underhill's Chair. This galleon carried a substantial amount of gold coins, silver place, and silver bullion. Incidentally, the Cosport Church, located on **Star Island**, was constructed partly of timbers from this galleon.

Spanish Galleon

On the western side of the island there was once an old fort that was protected by nine cannons. Although the cannons have since been removed, the area of the fort itself is a good metal detecting site for relics, coins, and the like.

Silver Ship Disaster

In the 18th century, **Appledore Island** was the scene of a terrible silver ship disaster in which sailors managed to get ashore with a substantial amount of the bullion that had been aboard. The history of the sailors has been lost in the years, but there have been many cases of people finding silver coins on or near the ledges along the eastern side of the island.

Blackbeard Buries Treasure on Smuttynose

Smuttynose Island is the site of Blackbeard's buried treasure of silver bars and pieces-of-eight. The silver bars are believed to be the same ones found by a Captain Samuel Haley. Haley found five large silver bars while building a sea wall for **Malaga Island**. So if, indeed, those were the silver bars Blackbeard buried, then the pieces-of-eight are yet to be found.

Shipwreck on Smuttynose Yields Gold and Silver

In January 1813 a ship named *Conception* out of Cadiz, Spain, was far off its course in a storm and slid by Cedar Island and crashed ashore at Southeast Point, **Smuttynose Island**. Her cargo of dried fruits, almonds, bales of broadcloth, and a treasure of gold and silver went down with her crew. Considerable gold and silver was discovered shortly after the wreck on the low-tide shore. Also found was a silver pocket watch inscribed with the initials P. S.

Pirate John Quelch Secrets Treasure on White Island

White Island, which is one mile southwest of Star Island, also holds treasure buried by John Quelch and probably others at several locations on the island.

How much of Quelch's treasure is buried on the **Isles of Shoals** is open to conjecture. *Life Magazine*, in 1950, stated that $100,000 was buried there,

John Quelch's Pirate Flag

about half of which has been recovered. In "1001 Lost, Buried, or Sunken Treasures", the authoritative F. L. Coffman said that Quelch's crew secreted $275,000 on **Star Island** and established several other caches on **White Island**.

Originally a pirate hunter, John Quelch turned pirate when the opportunity presented itself. In July 1703, he signed aboard the brigantine *Charles of Boston*, which was outfitted as a privateer to sail against the French in Nova Scotia and Newfoundland waters. The captain of the boat was a man named Daniel Plowman.

Captain Plowman was unhappy, however, with the caliber of the crew which was recruited to man the newly-built, eighty-ton craft. To make matters worse, he was taken ill just before the ship was set to sail.

Anthony Holding, one of the crew's ringleaders, assumed command. He locked the ailing captain in his cabin and ordered the ship out to sea. Once underway, the crew chose John Quelch to be the captain, probably because he had the most knowledge of navigation. Instead of sailing northeast to battle the French ships, the *Charles* now set a course to the south on a search for plunder in the Caribbean and the Spanish Main. Sometime after Quelch had assumed command, Captain Plowman was thrown overboard, but whether dead or alive is not known.

Captain Sent Overboard

During the next three months Quelch made nine captures, five brigantines, a small sloop, two fishing boats, and a ship of about two hundred tons. These vessels were the property of the subjects of the King of Portugal, now an ally of the Queen of England. From these ships Quelch secured rich booty including a hundred-weight of gold dust, gold, and silver coins to the value of over one thousand pounds, ammunition, small arms, and a great quantity of fine fabrics, provisions, and rum. By attacking these ships, Quetch became a pirate, and the English Navy was on the watch for him.

Quelch arrived back at Marblehead, Massachusetts, where he was eventually arrested. However, between the time of his arrival and his arrest, he and several members of his crew managed to make their way to **Star Island** and **White Island** and bury large sums of money which they had obtained while in the Caribbean.

Quelch was arrested and sentenced to death by hanging. On June 30, 1704, he was hung at the foot of Fleet Street in Boston, Massachusetts.

The Legend of Pirate Sandy Gordon's White Isle Treasure

Captain Sandy Gordon, a pirate who buried a huge treasure sometime between 1715 and 1718 on **White Island** has been best described as both mean and greedy. **White Island** is one of nine small outcroppings of rock which are the Isles of Shoals and are found about ten miles off the shores of both Maine and New Hampshire.

Gordon went to sea from his home in Scotland while still a boy. The first record of his nautical career was as a ship's carpenter aboard the *Porpoise,* an armed merchantman commanded by Captain John Herring. The captain was commissioned to capture Algerian corsairs who were creating havoc with British shipping in the area of the Barbary Coast.

Captain Has Daughter Aboard

It was against all nautical protocols of the day, but Captain Herring took his beautiful eighteen-year-old daughter Martha on this mission rather than leave her alone at home.

Captain's Daughter

The *Porpoise* was not out of London but a few days when young Gordon began to make serious advances toward the golden-haired young maiden. Captain Herring soon caught wind of this and told Gordon to back off or face the venom of the cat-o-nine-tails.

The young ship's carpenter heeded this warning for a few days, but Martha's beauty attracted him like a powerful magnet. In fact, it was not long thereafter that Herring trapped Gordon alone with the girl in the captain's cabin.

The father was furious. Seizing the young seaman by the throat, he threw him sprawling upon the deck and sentenced him to seventy-two lashes upon his bare back. In addition, he was clapped into irons and interred in the ships hold for thirty days to meditate over his perfidy.

When he finally returned to duty, Sandy went about his appointed tasks quietly and diligently, but this was only on the surface. Clandestinely, he was plotting a bold mutiny with certain unsavory members of the crew. As soon as a majority of the hands were ready to challenge Captain Herring, the conspiracy was ripe.

Mutiny on the Porpoise

Gordon selected a dark night when he was on watch. At a shot from Gordon's pistol, the mutineers seized control of the *Porpoise*, overwhelming Captain Herring and the loyal crewmen. The surprised master was hauled from his cabin and bound to a gun.

The punishment that Captain Herring had so recently meted out to Sandy was all too indelibly printed on the young sailor's mind. Seizing a lash, he evened the score then and there with seventy-two strokes upon the master's back. After several such beatings, spaced one hour apart, the Captain finally died and Gordon threw his body overboard.

Become a Pirate or be Thrown Overboard

At this point, Sandy locked Martha in the captain's cabin and forbade anyone to approach her. He gave everyone on board a choice, either turn pirate or be thrown overboard. The choice was easy to make. It was at this time that Gordon showed his greedy nature. His policy on this pirate ship was that there would be no division of plunder, as was the custom among buccaneers. All profits would be his. One slight concession was made, that the men would be paid wages twenty-five percent higher than those on merchant ships.

Fired as Captain, Expelled from the Ship

Now under the Jolly Roger, the ship sailed for some time off the coast of Scotland, capturing several valuable prizes. However, the crew grew exasperated with Gordon's reaping all the profits while they risked life and limb. So it was not unexpected when they rebelled against Gordon. As a result, the pirates set Sandy and Martha adrift in a small boat and let them row for the Scottish coast. The two managed to find an old farm house as their home in the desolate coastal area.

Enter Blackbeard

It was at that time that the rascally Captain Edward Teach, called Blackbeard, Thatch, Tinch, or Drummond, and a small party visited this lonely shore in search of water, food, and liquor. When Teach came upon Gordon's humble abode, the latter did not have much to offer except lurid tales of his prowess as an adventurer and one-time pirate.

Come aboard my ship, said Teach, and I'll see how good a pirate you are. If you are as good as your boasting, I'll see you outfitted, and maybe we can do business together.

Soon after Gordon came aboard, the pirates sighted a richly laden East Indian ship, homeward bound for London. Harold T. Wilkins in Pirate Treasure relates that the merchant ship put up a furious defense.

Gordon fought like a wild beast with cutlass and pistol until the merchantman's deck was clear of defenders. When the prize was finally secure, Teach slapped Gordon on the back and announced, Good work, lad. By your bravery today ye shown that ye deserve to be skipper of this prize. But mind you, all loot will be shared with the crew.

Made Captain by Blackbeard

Thus it was that Gordon renamed the ship the *Flying Scot*, and he and Teach set sail for the Spanish Main. This cruise was highly successful with both ships being well loaded with plunder. Eventually the two ships parted company, with an agreement to meet again at a future date among the Isles of Shoals.

Stopped to Pick up his Girlfriend

Following this agreement, Gordon sailed back to Scotland where he dropped anchor near his coastal farmhouse. He went ashore in a small boat and returned to his ship in the darkness of that night with the beautiful Martha in his arms. She was bound and carried kicking and screaming to the ship. Not a good way to begin the long journey to America.

On the cruise to America, the *Flying Scot* sighted a great Spanish galleon and gave chase. As the pirates drew near, the Spaniard let go with a broadside which was inaccurate enough to cause little damage. Meanwhile, the *Flying Scot* lived up to her name and pulled alongside the Spaniard. Grappling hooks were thrown to link the ships together, and then the buccaneers swarmed aboard their victim like a host of angry hornets.

Gordon played it safe and stood on his quarterdeck until his men had the situation well in hand. Now the time had come for him to leap aboard the merchantman and take the Spanish captain as his prisoner.

The galleons captain proved to be a very stubborn individual, but, after some highly persuasive measures, he revealed the amount of treasure on board and the secret places in which it was stored, and then he was thrown overboard. Gordon took more than a million dollars worth of gold and silver out of the Spanish vessel.

His crew Buried their Loot on Star Island

The *Flying Scot* arrived at the Isles of Shoals several weeks before Captain Teach. Landing at **Star Island**, Gordon ordered a division of the treasure to be made. When this had been accomplished, *the crew broke up into several small groups to bury their shares of loot.*

What of Captain Gordon and the fair Martha? They took up residence a short distance away on **White Island**. Sandy had a small cottage built for them there, and it was near the cottage that he buried his treasure.

How much did he bury? This is anyone's guess, but most authorities agree that it was an amount of considerable value.

In time, Captain Teach arrived on the scene, and there was more burying of treasure. Teach is alleged to have cached as much as $300,000 on **Star Island**. Both he and Gordon held several conferences at this time, and when it was amicably agreed to dissolve their partnership, Teach took off for the Spanish Main.

Unfortunate Case of Mistaken Identity

A week or two later, a lookout spied a sail on the horizon. The lure for more booty was great, so Gordon hastily assembled the crew and lifted anchor. The strange sail turned out to be a British man-o-war on a hunt for pirates. A long and fierce conflict followed in which the British ship finally silenced Gordon's guns. The vessels were locked together for the last stage of the conflict, when a tremendous explosion rent the air, strewing the sea with the fragments of both ships.

Stung to madness by defeat and knowing that, if taken alive, he would be gallows bait, Sandy Gordon fired the *Flying Scots* magazine, sending himself and his merry men to eternity. His girlfriend and his treasure remained **White Island**.

The Blood Red Rubies of Boon Island

September 25, 1710, the English ship *Nottingham* departed her home port of London and headed for New England. The 120 ton Galley was crewed by fourteen men and carried ten cannon and was commanded by Captain Jonathan Dean. Her cargo consisted of: loads of cordwood, butter and cheese from Ireland, plus one very special cargo, a packet of twelve blood-red rubies in the charge of agent Winthrop Sloan, the sole passenger aboard.

Only in America

They were sold to a wealthy French aristocrat, the Count de Florent, on the condition that they be rendered into matching items of jewelry that matched those of a large pendant and brooch he owned. The Count insisted that the only person in the world capable of performing the task was a goldsmith living in America so off to America went the precious rubies.

The rubies were quite large and carefully packed into an oblong metal box measuring one inch by one-half inch by twelve inches. The box was then securely stored in the ships iron safe. The stones estimated market value today would be well in excess of $1,500,000.

As the *Nottingham* approached New England she was firmly gripped by blinding December snow storm and a full-force gale. The heavy wind threatened to capsize the ship, so Captain Dean ordered the sails dropped. However, before the task could be completed, a huge wave lifted the galley and plunged it against the eastern end of the jagged, exposed rock known as **Boon Island**.

Miraculously everyone had survived the sinking, including the passenger Sloan. As the splintered *Nottingham* and her ruby treasure vanished beneath the boiling waves, the men settled into prayer, grateful for their very survival.

Stranded on Boon Island

They had spent twenty seven days on the rock known as **Boon Island** before they were rescued. The men were weak and frozen after nearly a month without fresh water, little food, and no fire in the blistering cold. They were walking skeletons. All had frost bite and frozen limbs but they were still alive although many had to have limbs amputated

So there remains, somewhere near **Boon Island** near **Star Island**, the scattered wreckage of the *Nottingham,* close nearby, is an iron safe containing a fortune in rare rubies waiting for some lucky person to find them.

Duck Island Lone Survivor Tells of Money Chest

In March 1876, only one person survived a shipwreck on an unidentified brig that crashed behind **White Island**. The schooner *Birkmyre* hit **Duck Island** in March 1875, losing two of its crew and a substantial amount of money in a chest which has not been recovered

Appledore, in the Isles of Shoals, was another such a hiding-place, and Kidd put one of his crew to death that he might haunt the place and frighten searchers from their quest. For years no fisherman could be induced to land there after nightfall, for did not an islander once encounter "Old Bab" on his rounds, with a red ring around his neck, a frock hanging about him, phosphorescence gleaming from his body, who peered at the intruder with a white and dreadful face, and nearly scared him to death?

Treasure in Casco Bay

Where might it be found?

Jewell Island Captain Kidd, fearing imminent capture, is said to have put ashore and buried his treasure on **Jewell Island** off Portland Head. He then marked the spot with either a square flat rock or reversed compass carved on a tree. He is reported to have made a map for finding his hoard of gold and jewels. The map has not been found.

A second pirate and smuggler, Captain Chase, is part of **Jewell Island** pirate lore. It is said that Chase would post lanterns to lure innocent ships unfamiliar with Maine's waters onto the rocky shore. Chase and his men would then plunder the wreck scooping up anything of value and murdering any surviving crew.

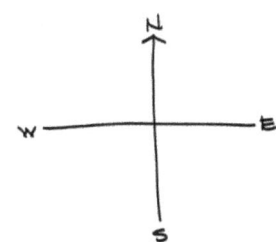

Jewel Island is the only site where actual excavations have been undertaken and with which many detailed stories are associated.

On **Bailey Island**, also in **Casco Bay,** there is a well-authenticated story of pirate treasure **actually having been found** in the 1850s. A farmer named John Wilson was duck hunting on the island when, in an attempt to retrieve a fallen bird, he slipped into a crevice between two ledges. In his scramble to climb out, he uncovered an **iron pot filled with pieces of Spanish gold**. He exchanged these for $12,000 in coin of the realm, a comfortable fortune at that time.

Matinicus –

Often referred to as the **pirate island** because; in the spring of 1717 the pirate ships *Anne* and *Fisher,* being survivors of the fierce storm of April 26, 1717 that sank pirate Samuel Bellamy's treasure laden ship the *Whydah* off of a Cape Cod beach, used the island as a base to attack vessels in the area as they awaited Bellamy's arrival.

While the pirates waited at **Matinicus**:

> "....... they took a sloop belonging to Colonel [Stephen] Minot, one shallop belonging to Capt. [John] Lane and three Schooners. They brought the Sloop and Shallop and (as we are informed) the sails and compasses of the 3 schooners to **Menhagen [Monhegan]**, whereupon they manned the last mentioned Sloop with ten hands..."

The pirates departed the area on May 9, 1717, on the 25-ton sloop formerly belonging to Colonel Minot, with a pirate crew of 19.

On **Damariscotta Island**, near Kennebec, Maine, is a lake of salt water, which, like dozens of shallow ones in this country, is locally reputed to be bottomless. Yet Kidd was believed to have sunk some of his valuables there, and to have guarded against the entrance of boats by means of a chain hung from rock to rock at the narrow entrance, bolts on either side showing the points of attachment, while ring bolts were thought to have been driven for the purpose of tying buoys, thus marking the spots where the chests went down. This island, too, has been held in fear as haunted ground.

Cedar Ledges east of **Ram Island** in Casco Bay, three kettles of gold coins were found on Thanksgiving Day, 1852, and more may still be there.

Haskell Island is located near **Harpswell Neck** and is reported to be one of several places along the Maine coast that Captain Kidd is supposed to have hidden some of his treasure. According to the "Folklore of Maine" in the Library of the Maine Historical Society, the Haskell brothers, one brother took ill and the other rowed to the mainland to get medical help.

While he was gone a band of bounty hunters came to the island and found Captain Kidd's treasure but were discovered by the ailing Haskell brother. To keep their secret the bounty hunters killed and slashed the Haskell brother to pieces in an attempt to make it look as though the island's many cats had done the gruesome deed. Did the bounty hunters find all of Captain Kidd's hidden treasure?

Cliff Island was once the home of a tough, old salvager called Captain Keiff. He lived alone in a log hut on the island. His favorite way to wreck ships was to tie a lantern to his horse's neck, then ride up and down the shoreline. Ships at sea would be misguided by this light and be wrecked on the reefs and ledges that surrounded the island. Keiff

Ship Lured onto rocks

would kill any survivors of the wrecks, and then salvage the cargo. In those days, while it wasn't encouraged, illegal salvaging was condoned, and no questions were asked when someone sold salvaged goods.

Keiff is supposed to have made a fortune in his nefarious occupation. There is a place on the island still known as **Keiffs Gardens**. Local stories say that somewhere on the island a large part of Keiffs money is still buried. This is quite possible, since he had no family and lived alone with very few ways to spend money, as the wrecked ships supplied him with most of his needs.

Dixie Bull, an English sea captain descended from an aristocratic family, was the first pirate known to prey upon shipping off the northeastern colonies, especially along the rocky coast of Maine. Some of his hidden hoards have contributed to the traditions of pirates and buried treasure along the New England coast.

One of his treasures was reputed to be worth $400,000 at the time of its burial on **Damariscove Island**. If found today, its value could be worth $4,000,000 or more in today's dollars.

Another of his hoards is supposed to have been buried on **Cushing Island**, also off the Maine coast. Neither trove is known to have been recovered.

Bull was a native of London who came to Boston in 1631. He was associated with Sir Ferdinando Gorges in development of a large land grant east of Agamonticus at York, Maine. He rapidly adapted to the rugged life of the New Worlds wilderness, becoming a trader in beaver pelts with the Indians.

Pinnace under sail

In June 1631, while trading in the **Penobscot Bay** area, Bull was attacked by a roving band of Frenchmen in a pinnace, or small sailing ship. They seized his sloop and stock of coats, rugs, blankets, biscuits, etc. This same band captured the Plymouth Company's **Castine** trading post which was filled with other valuable loot.

Trader Bull, fired by a desire for revenge, assembled 20 men to prey upon French shipping in an effort to recoup his loss. Their attempts were unsuccessful, for the French had temporarily ceased their raids. Bull's food and supplies were running low, so he attacked and plundered three small English vessels in order to keep operating.

These attacks put him in serious trouble with the Crown, and he became desperate. His next escapade was later in 1632, when he sailed into the harbor of **Pemaquid,** sacked the trading post and nearby dwellings, and escaped with $2,500 in both.

There was little resistance to the attack, but while loading goods aboard his sloop, someone on shore fired a musket and Bulls second in command was struck in the chest, killing him. Until then, many of the crew had considered piracy a lark. Now it suddenly became deadly serious business.

Early in February 1633, three of Bull,s crew secretly returned to their Maine homes. They said Bull had sailed eastward and joined the French, his former enemies. Another statement by a Captain Roger Clap indicated that Bull eventually returned to England. His destiny is lost in the maze of history. One version says that he was finally captured and hung at Tyburn, England.

Bull's fate will probably never be known. The fate of his buried treasure on **Cushing and Damariscove Islands** may be determined by a skillful treasure hunter.

Pond Island

Early in the 18th century it is reported that a conscripted sailor escaped from the pirate Captain Lowe's ship "Don Pedro." The ship was carrying a load of jewelry, gold and silver from Mexico to Spain. Somewhere off the coast of New York the pirate's ship was spotted by a British frigate which chased it all the way to Casco Bay where they lost sight of it in a dense fog.

Pond Island Light

The pirates came ashore on Pond Island and are said to have buried their treasure on the island planning to return for it once they were free of the pursuing frigate. The loot, reportedly worth $100,000 in the 1700s, must be worth multi millions today.

Lowe never returned to recover the loot, and was executed by a French court for piracy. A pot of gold coins was found by a farmer on **Pond Island** so Edward Lowe or other pirates may have regularly hid treasure on this island.

Another Account of Pond Island Treasure

The pirate Edward Lowe is believed to have buried a huge sum of gold coins, silver bars, and jewels in the **Harpswell** area at both **Haskell Island** at the **South Harpswell Neck** and at the edge of a pond on **Pond Island** in Casco Bay east of Harpswell.

In 1723, he attacked the Spanish ship Don Pedro del Montclova that was traveling from Havana to Spain, commandeered the treasure, and sank the ship. When a British gunboat began pursuing them, Captain Lowe and his men hauled the treasure ashore at the south end of **Pond Island** in three longboats, and then carried it to the edge of a large pond on the northeast side of the island and tossed the chests, bars of silver, and kegs into the water.

Orrs Island- The story is that while Captain Kit was plowing his field he struck what reports described as a "pot of gold." He and his eleven children lived the good life thereafter.

Jewell Island, in Casco Bay, is supposed to be one of the places where **Captain Kidd** buried his treasure. Whether Kidd ever visited the island is unknown, but there is a story, backed up by considerable evidence, that a Captain Jonathan Chase **found a large treasure** on the island, killing his helper and burying him during the recovery. No record of what happened to Chase or the money can be found.

Great Chebeague Island, reached by ferry from **Falmouth to Portland**, is the second-largest island in **Casco Bay**.

In the 1860s, an old sailor said that in his pirate days he had been one of a pirate crew which many years before had buried a great treasure here. He began digging in a secluded part of the island. One day, a young islander offered to assist him. When the offer was curtly refused, the islander leaped over the rope with which the old man had enclosed the spot where he was digging; whereupon the treasure seeker, in a voice quaking with anger, cried, I call on God and you people to witness that within a year this young fool will be tied in knots, even as I could tie this rope.

No one remembers now whether any treasure was found, but a short time later, the young man was soaked while fishing. He was confined to his bed with an agonizing malady which drew up his arms and legs as if tied in knots, and when he died, soon afterward, it was necessary to break the bones of his limbs in order to get his body into the casket.

John's Island

One might wonder if there is any truth to the story of treasure on **Johns Island, in Casco Bay**. Many stories cling to this little island, which is famed as being the summer home of the Lauder family and Gene Tunney. Tradition has it that there was a large frame tavern on the north end of the island, a hangout for seamen. One of these was a Portuguese who never did any work, but always had plenty of **gold and silver** to spend when he appeared from parts unknown.  This went on for years. Finally, he died in a foreign land, but before he breathed his last, he gave a friend a map of **Johns Island**, showing the location of a **hidden well near the tavern**. At the bottom of the well, he said, gold and silver would be found because I helped put it there from the pirate craft *Dare Devil*, commanded by **Dixie Bull**. Searches have been made for this well, but without success.

Treasure in Penobscot Bay

Deer Isle, Was the New York Astor family's fortune actually founded upon the Pirate Captain William Kidd's treasure found in an iron box (with the initials WK chiseled on the lid) hidden on the property of Mr. Frederick Law Olmsted. Olmstead was a famous landscape architect and designer of New York's *Central Park* and Boston's *"Emerald Necklace."* Is there more treasure to be found on Deer Isle?

Just before Captain Kidd was to be hanged in 1710 and, after a whispered conference with his wife, Kidd was seen handing a small piece of past board her. This card bore the mysterious figures "44106818."

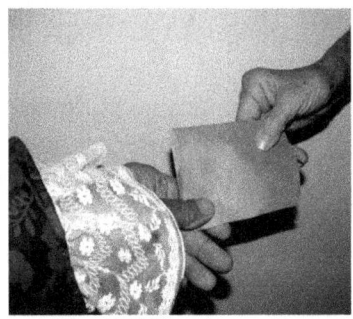

Capt Kidd passes note

Could the numbers indicate the longitude 4410 and latitude 6818 and the exact location of the remainder of Captain Kidd's treasure? The latitude for Deer Isle is exactly 4410! Plus, a cave on the Olmsted estate's latitude 6813, very close to the 6818 scribbled on Captain Kidd's final writing before he was hung.

Monroe Island Located off of Owl's Point State Park in Penobscot Bay. For many years this island was reportedly used by pirates and thieves. Treasures are reportedly been hidden all over the island.

Oak Island located in Penobscot Bay. According to the book "Folklore of Maine," an elderly blind man is reported to have experienced a dream where a barrel of gold rolled out of a cave on a cliff into a pond below. His description matched that of a place on Oak Island where a pond lay below a cliff with a cave. The pond was dragged for a week but the gold filled barrel was not found. There are those who still believe that gold is there waiting to be found.

Great Duck Island is a 237 acre island located at sea approximately 10 miles south of **Mt Desert Island**. The northeast end of the island consists of cliffs and ledges, but ironically contains the only "all-weather" landing spot.

William Bigenho, who purchased the island in 1951, had identified it as the island on a 16th or 17th century "treasure map." His daughter later reported that her parents discovered a treasure consisting of gold, silver, and various artifacts. They were lead to the site of the treasure by a combination of the map and various signs carved on rocks, perhaps including a reversed compass.

Bucksport area

Jean Vincent de lAbadie, Baron de St. Castine, was a French nobleman who inherited land on **Penobscot Bay** in what is now the state of Maine. He took possession in 1665 and ran a successful trading post at the village of Pentagoet for nearly 25 years, amassing a fortune.

In 1840, Captain Stephen Grindle and his son Samuel were hauling logs to the **Narrows**, (an area near **Bucksport**) about six miles from the village, when they found a coin, a French crown. The pair dug until dark, recovering 20 more coins. It was in late November, and during the night a severe blizzard struck, so digging was suspended until the spring of 1841.

Returning in the spring, the Grindles dug up nearly **500 coins** from France, Spain, South America, Portugal, Holland, England, and Massachusetts. Was this the de Castine hoard, missing for 137 years?

The collection also contained **150 Pine Tree shillings and sixpence** dated 1652. This was the first coinage struck in the colonies. The Pine Tree shillings are valued up to **$2,000 each**.

It was reported in 1855 that a man named Connolly, another **Narrows** resident, found an old chest with the remains of clothing and other goods.

Records show Baron de St. Castine fled with **six money chests**. Thus far, only one has reportedly been found. Records further indicate that a year before the Barons flight, a French visitor had estimated the treasure to be worth $200,000. Over three hundred years have passed. What is the value of those five missing chests today?

Sunken Treasure aboard Circus Ship

For those interested in sunken treasure, somewhere in **Penobscot Bay**, Maine, not far from **Vinalhaven**, are the charred remains of the 164 foot side-wheeler *Royal Tar*, and her treasure chest of **$35,000 in gold** and **silver.**

This is the story of a vessel that caught fire east of Fox Island in **Penobscot Bay** and later drifted off and sank. The ship carried 85 passengers and a menagerie of circus animals, 32 persons and all of the animals perished. The ship left St. John, New Brunswick and was headed toward Portland, ME in the year 1886.

A circus, returning to the States after a highly successful summer tour of New Brunswick, chartered the *Royal Tar* for the voyage home. The circus was almost too big to fit on the ship. Several of the *Royal Tars* lifeboats were removed in order to fit the troupe aboard.

The ship sailed for Portland, Maine, on October 21, 1836, riding very low in the water, her decks crowded with circus animals, including a gigantic Indian elephant.

As the steamer lay at anchor about two miles off the **Fox Island** thoroughfare in **Penobscot Bay**, the ship burst into flames. The fire grew with lightning speed and soon was beyond control and the captain ordered the few lifeboats filled and lowered.

Seven hours after the fire had begun; the *Royal Tar* sank beneath the waves. It is estimated that, in the meantime, she had drifted some 20 miles, as the captain had pulled the anchor.

The $35,000 in the pursers safe was untouched by anyone during the fire. It is understandable that all concerned had to abandon the ship too hastily to think about saving the money. At least, this was the report of all those questioned following the disaster.

So the treasure was still on board the *Royal Tar* when she sank, and the facts seem to indicate that it is still there, on the bottom of Penobscot Bay with an **estimated value, in today's dollars, of $3,500,000.**

Treasure in Boothbay

This short story has a mystery concerning a treasure location that has never been reported solved. **Outer Heron Island, Maine**, lies a few miles offshore from **Boothbay Harbor**.

Around 1900, two young men came to **Outer Heron Island** from New York. They had a map of the island showing where a chest of pirate gold was supposedly buried. The two never revealed how this map came into their possession. With a specially constructed auger that could be lengthened indefinitely by adding sections of iron rod, they started boring near a lone, grotesquely-shaped spruce tree on the highest point of the island.

Pirate's Map?

After a month of constant work, and at a depth of 30 feet, the auger brought up oaken chips. They penetrated this, and the bit came up with particles of what seemed to be gold. The two then hired two Italian laborers and excavated a 30-foot shaft. At this depth, a 6-foot oak plank was found, and that was all. The gold had come from a copper spike which the auger point had rapped.

The mystery is how did a copper spike and a six-foot plank get 30 feet underground, unless some kind of excavating had been done years before? No report of any treasures being found in the area can be located.

Swan's Island, located in the Kennebec River. Is reported to be the site of another pirate cache.

Mid Coast Maine

Fort Pemaguid - The Pirate Dixie Bull began his piratical career by converting his trading sloop into a pirate ship and attacking the fort and got loot valued at 500 pounds.

This little-known treasure was found by accident and then lost again and has never been rediscovered. **Manana Island** is off the middle coast of Maine. Around 1900, several fishermen stopped their boat at this island to relax. They decided to play a game of soccer. When a wild kick was made by one of the crewmembers, the captain of the group ran to retrieve the ball.

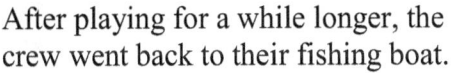

As he picked up the ball, he noticed rusty metal sticking out of the sand. He dug the sand from around the object, and saw that it was an old iron pot filled with coins. Since he was out of sight of his crew, he stuck the pot into a nearby rock crevice, intending to come back for it later.

After playing for a while longer, the crew went back to their fishing boat.
The captain made an excuse to stay behind for a short time. Returning to what he thought was the crevice where he had put the **pot of coins**, he was amazed that he could not find the right one. Deciding that part of the coins would be better than none, the captain called his crew and told them what he had done.

The entire company spent several hours in search of the coins, but were never able to find them. As far as is known, somewhere on **Manana Island**, stuck in a rock crevice, there is a cache of coins waiting for a lucky treasure hunter.

Macias Region

Frequented by Several Pirates

Captain Rhodes

If you are ever in the areas of the coastal town of **Machias,** you will hear tales of loot hidden by the notorious pirate, **Captain Rhodes**. He roamed this shore in 1675, using the sheltered inlet of the **Machias River** as a hideout and a place for careening his ship.

Captains Harry Thompson and Starbird

Another **Machias** area treasure is also stashed along **Starbirds Creek**. Years ago, Captain Harry Thompson and another buccaneer named Starbird frequently used the entrance to the **Machias River** as a rendezvous between voyages. As a consequence, they used a nearby creek, named for Starbird, to cache their plunder. Thompson was said to have marked some trees and to have drawn a crude map to aid his children in locating this trove, but they apparently misinterpreted the clues, for they dug without success.

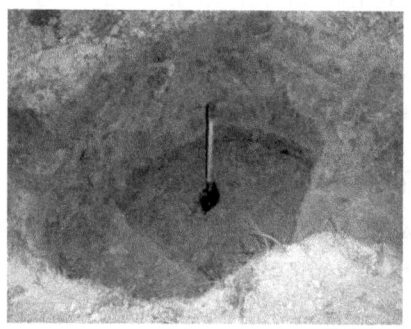

The Brothers Flynn

In the same general area, **Brothers Island**, named for two brothers called Flynn, is reputedly a hiding place for their trove. However, information concerning this cache is not easy to establish.

Pirates Samuel Bellamy and Paulsgrave Williams

There reportedly is a hidden underground vault containing pirate treasure in the vicinity of the **Machias River**. Legend says that the Pirate, Black Bellamy built the vault beneath his wooden fort on the river. The fort is now gone, but it was known to be located near the bridge on State route A1.

Other version reports the treasure mouth of the **Machias River** is not where the two pirates had their stronghold, but further upriver. They did dig a subterranean treasure house, but it was not inside the fort. There is little doubt but that the vault holds a large hoard of what we call treasure today.

After looting a number of ships, the pirates arrived at a destination selected by Captain Bellamy, the only navigator on board. The spot was near the mouth of the **Machias River**, far from any civilized community at that time. It was here that Bellamy and Williams put their plan into action. The cargo had to be hidden very well before they sailed to continue their pirating.

Bellamy's Jolly Roger

A large vault was excavated to serve as a treasure house and their treasure secreted. When all of this was done, and the *Whydah* had been overhauled, Bellamy and Williams set sail again. After several forays, the treasure house was filled.

The headquarters of Bellamy and Williams, near the mouth of the **Machias River**, has disappeared. But somewhere nearby is hidden one of the richest pirate caches in North America, one that has never been reported found.

Black Sam Bellamy, the Robin hood of the Sea, had the stereotype Jolly Roger.

Monhegan Island,

Being located miles out to sea off the mainland, Monhegan Island is a natural for pirates. Captain Bellamy, "the richest pirate," is said to have hidden some of his treasure "somewhere on the island"

Allagash Region

Lost Smuggling Fortune

A story treasure on the **Allagash River**, is that of Anse Hanley. During the early days of timber-cutting, the lumber companies were constantly in trouble with squatters. These people would carve out a small homestead on company land, then hint to the owners that if they were forced to move, a forest fire might start that would destroy millions of dollars worth of timber. In most cases, the squatters stayed on the property.

One such land parasite was Anse Hanley. Around 1900, Hanley came to **Fort Kent**, accompanied by his wife and two children.

After obtaining supplies, he moved up the **Allagash River** in Arrostook County, where he squatted. During the next few years, Hanley engaged in making whiskey for sale to the loggers.

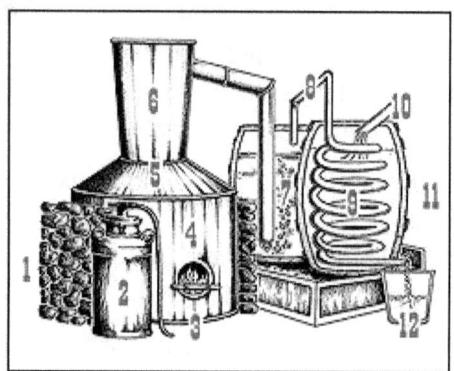

Whiskey Still Diagram

It was said of his homemade product, if a man can drink it and come back for more, he will live forever. Hanley also sold farm products and engaged in smuggling whiskey, guns, and cigarettes from Canada, which he sold to American sportsmen and hunters. When Hanley died, he left a rumored **$60,000**, some of which he had hidden before his death, and it has never be found.

Inland Treasures

Many gold and silver coins have been discovered buried in the ground all over the state of Maine, mostly by farmers and gardeners. There were no banks or other institutional places for the safe keeping of valuables. Therefore, folks would bury their cash and other valuables to keep them safe.

Naturally few would disclose the location of their stashes to friends or even family so, when accidental and sudden death or debilitating sickness struck, the treasure remained buried and unknown.

Pot of Gold

Reports of such treasure being accidentally uncovered are often kept secret and not divulged. A few reports of buried treasure finds are chronicled here.

Richmond Island, offshore from **Cape Elizabeth**, a treasure of gold and silver coins was found by a farmer and his two sons as they plowed their field. They hit a pot filled with gold and silver coins dated from 1588 to 1649 and a gold ring. The amazing discovery was chronicled in the Eastern Argus on May 24, 1855.

Portland – An influential politician's gardener digs up a 1579 silver sixpence at the State Street address.

A vacant lot at the corners of Vaughan and Brackett streets in Portland yields a 1655 "Leg Dollar." It was so named because of the one legged military figure shown on the face of the coin.

Saco - William Edgecomb was working in his garden on the **Ferry Road** in Saco in the spring of 1931 when he dug up a gold coin dated 1723.

Biddeford

In the summer of 1931 two gardeners while transplanting flowers discovered 63 Spanish gold and silver coins scattered around in the dirt.

The Biddeford Journal described one of the coins: "Elie T. Labbe took one of the coins in a splendid state of preservation bearing the date 1805 to a local bank this morning where he was told that it was a $1 Spanish coin of the reign of Charles IV of Spain. He was also informed that the value of the coin at this time is $65."

Spanish coin of Charles IV 1805

Labbe told the Journal reporter that he intended to do some more digging before totaling up his buried treasure, but he didn't believe it would ever amount to enough for him to be able to retire from the florist business.

He also made a plea for help from local historians in solving the mystery of how Spanish coins might have come to be buried on his land at 200 Pool St., **Biddeford**

Biddeford Pool was attacked by the British man-of-war *Bulwark* on June 16, 1814. English Frigate Bulwark attacked Biddeford Pool. The Harmoine, Catherine and Equator were sunk. One ship in the stocks (unknown name) was burned and one ship the Victory was stolen for ransom of $6000.

John Staples Locke wrote of the incident in his 1880 book, "Shores of Saco Bay." "Messengers were dispatched through the country on horseback, to alarm the inhabitants. All the men capable of bearing arms left their fields and hastened towards the Pool. Women and children fled to the woods with their valuables. One aged lady tells of taking the silver of a wealthy **Saco** family and burying it in the woods near where is now the **Eastern Depot**."

Carpenter Ridge Diamonds

In the 1850's, when diamonds were being smuggled from Canada into the U.S., a man emerged from the woods east of **Portage Lake** and claimed he had buried a leather pouch full of diamonds close to **Portage Lake on Carpenter Ridge** in the grave where he buried his daughter after she died during their long trip. It is not known if he placed a marker on her grave or not. They were on their way south to Bangor to meet a boat that would take them to Boston. There is a trail from the main road that now that leads to the summit of **Carpenter Ridge.**

Egyptian Mummies

There is an unusual treasure that is probably still where it was stored, about ten miles southwest of **Portland** waiting to be found.

Mummy

To some people the idea of searching for **Egyptian mummies** might seem sacrilegious, but remember that the mummies have already been taken from their original graves, transported to the United States, and are worth, on today's collectors market, in excess of $12,000 each. Here is the story.

In 1857, and thereafter for several years, newspaper publishers in this country faced a severe shortage of rags, which were necessary to add strength and body to wood fibers used in paper sheets. As the shortage of rags increased, large numbers of small newspapers went out of business.

Augustus Stanwood, a printer in **Portland,** Maine, was greatly affected by this rag shortage. Realizing that he would go broke, Stanwood looked around for a much-needed source of this ever-increasing shortage of fiber. One night, while drinking with a sea captain, Stanwood told him of his troubles. The sailing captain suggested using the cloth wrappings of mummies. (At this time the Egyptian grave sites were being exploited, and artifacts, coffins, and mummies were being sold by the thousands throughout the world.)

Augustus made a deal with the ship's captain to obtain several dozen of these cloth-wrapped bodies. When the shipment arrived, Stanwood stored them on his property, in pits to preserve them, about **ten miles southwest of Portland**. During the next three to seven years, he used about half of the mummies, putting their linen and cotton wrappings into his paper grinders. The pulp made a very good grade of paper stock.

About this time the rag shortage let up because of the Civil War and the capture of huge stores of cotton by Union forces throughout the South. Thus, Stanwood did not need to use the rest of his mummies. After he tried to sell them and couldn't, Stanwood left the mummies in the pits he had dug on his property.

After Stanwood died, few people even remembered the mummies, and they are, as far as can be determined, still buried on the old Stanwood property, about ten miles southwest of **Portland,** Maine. If you aren't afraid of ghosts, this unusual treasure could be worth thousands of dollars today.

Paper Making

Native and Natural Treasure

Maine is home to the ores of most metals and the gemstones such as **tourmalines, beryl, amethyst, garnet, and topaz**. At least one mineral, **beryllonite**, has been found *nowhere outside Maine*, and this state has yielded the finest **emerald beryl** ever found in the United States. In mineral production, Maine stands about midway among the states, with the annual yield being valued at about **$6,000,000**. One-third of the state is still unexplored in respect to mineral resources, and only limited areas have received adequate investigation.

Tourmaline, from Newry, Maine mine

Of other metals, platinum and iridium are reported, although the possibility of obtaining them for commercial use is not yet clear. **Gold** is present in small quantities in a number of places. **Silver** is found in most of the lead and zinc localities, and the copper ores at **Bluehill.** That there are considerable bodies of lead and zinc of definite value has been known since they were first mined in 1860. Some **pure silver** has been mined at **Sullivan** and elsewhere.

More specific locations of different mineral sites can be obtained from the State Geology Department at Augusta, Maine.

Lost Silver Mine

The legend states that Indians under a Captain Sunday **mined silver** near the town of **Cornish, Cumberland County**. The place was marked by three small hills flanking the **Saco River** near its junction with the **Ossipee River**. The mined silver was stored and never used. After working the mine for several years, the Indians sold the land on which it was located to William Phillips, who spent the remainder of his life searching for the mine, but never found it.

Mother Lode of Gold in Southern Maine

Somewhere in the middle of **southwestern Maine, in Oxford County**, there exists a mother lode of gold beyond the wildest dreams of any treasure hunter. Pure conjecture? Not at all; that statement is based on solid fact and research.

Entrance to a Mine

For 50 years, concentrated efforts have been made by professional geologists to find the source of gold in **Oxford County's brooks, lakes, and ponds**. The precious metal is found everywhere, and platinum is found occasionally. At the present time, research is continuing in the **Wilson Mills** area, very close to the New Hampshire border. There is very definitely gold in them thar hills, particularly in the region of **Eustis.**

Swift River Gold

Near **Byron, the Swift River** and its many feeders have produced more **gold** than all of the other Maine regions combined. Anyone who can handle a pan will find small traces of the color if he is willing to spend the time. As many as a dozen persons can be seen panning the stream on any given day. A few do their prospecting by searching behind the stream on any given day. A few do their prospecting by searching behind the upturned stones and boulders where small nuggets sometimes collect.

Trappers have been finding a small amount of **gold** in the **Swift River** almost since the area was first opened to settlement. Within recent memory, over $7,000 of the yellow stuff was taken from among a jumbled pile of rocks at a bend in the river. Perley Whitney took several thousand dollars worth over a period of years from one of the branches. Two Boston vacationers panned almost $500 in two weeks time from one of the small brooks that flow into the **Swift River**.

Finding Relics and Old Coins

Recovering older more valuable coins plus holding in your hands different relics of the past will be something you will want to experience. Finding coins from the 17th, 18th and early 19th Century is a far greater thrill then you can imagine.

The answer to finding older sites is "Research!" Where can you find research material?

1-Old Maps - can be found in local libraries, local history books, they show old roads, abandoned railroad stations, many times school buildings and other points of interest that either no longer exist, or people have forgotten about.

2-Old Newspapers contain a wealth of information on almost every page Stories about holiday celebration on the town square park (May no longer exists) Carnival arriving in town (where did they set up?) and much more information.

3-Old Property Tax Records show where older houses, farms, service stations, interstate bus stops, taverns etc, once stood.

4-Local Historical Societies are a great resource containing valuable information on dozens of older happenings of your town from its very beginnings up till today.

5-Local Museums usually have displays of historical interest as well as many books on the area's history. Spend time with anyone that works in the museum, they generally are part "Historian."

6- Librarians can direct you to a wealth of information about your town. Libraries are the main "Depository" of information of all kinds,, many times having a number of items discussed above, "old maps, old books, old records, etc".

Finding Treasure on Beaches

Valuables found on the beach may have been dropped by a vacationer or washed ashore from a sunken ship. Beach hunting is probably the only form of treasure hunting where almost anyone can go and find items worth $100's or even $1,000's.

The following tips will help you become successful in beach and water treasure detecting:.

- **The areas where mothers splash around with their toddlers** - Suntan lotion, cool water and splashing often combine to loosen rings that find their way off fingers.

- **The areas where teens and adults tend to horse around:** suntan lotion and horseplay tends to result in items being lost.

- **The dry sand:** Where chairs and towels are laid out, volleyball nets, around concession stands

Found on the Beach

15 Best Treasure Hunting Sites

There are literally hundreds of places to find coins, rings, jewelry, gold, relics, and even real buried and hidden treasures.

The key, go where people have been, where they lived, where they worked and played. From as far back as you can find to today. **People lose coins, rings, jewelry, and other treasures everywhere they go.**

All sorts of valuables are lost or hidden for safekeeping. Many valuables and treasures are buried by owners who perhaps die and never come back to retrieve them. All these millions of coins and tens of thousands of dollars in rings and jewelry are out there waiting to be found!

Some of the best places to search:

1. Parks
2. Schoolyards, Playgrounds
3. Fairgrounds
4. Picnic Areas
5. Amusement Parks
6. Swimming Areas such as Lakes and Rivers
7. Seaside Beaches
8. Sand, Dirt or Grassy Parking Areas
9. Old Home Sites
10. Old School Sites
11. Under Grandstands and Bleachers
12. Churchyards
13. Stonewalls near old farmhouses
14. Cemeteries
15. Carnival Sites

Where to Find Gold in Maine

Coos Canyon

Maine is a very big state, and anyone who has driven around there knows just how huge it is. Lots and lots of trees (and moose of course)! But, there is also lots of gold to be found in Maine.

By far the most popular spot is in Byron at Coos Canyon along the Swift River and the East Branch of the Swift River. There is a Rock & Mineral shop there called Coos Canyon Rock & Gift. You can buy prospecting supplies there as well as learn panning techniques.

Coos Canyon, Byron, ME

Coos Canyon is a scenic, rocky gorge carved through bedrock by the Swift River. The Swift River is one of more than a half dozen streams and rivers in Maine known to harbor deposits of gold. According to the Maine Department of Conservation's Gold Fact Sheet, "Gold occurs in several geologic environments in Maine: in bedrock, in sediments that were eroded from bedrock by glaciers, and in stream deposits derived from either of these sources."

Location: Coos Canyon is located in the town of Byron, Maine, on Route 17. It will come up on your right as you're headed toward Rangeley on Route 17 West.

Admission: There is free parking available at the Coos Canyon site.

Pan for Gold: Bring your own panning equipment, or rent gear and take a quick lesson in panning at the Coos Canyon Rock & Gift Shop located, across Route 17 from Coos Canyon.

More Places to Find Gold

Here are some other locations as listed by the state of Maine:

River	Town	County
Swift River and its tributaries	Byron area	Oxford, Franklin
Sandy River	Madrid to New Sharon	Franklin
South Branch-Penobscot River	Sandy Bay; Bald Mtn; Prentiss	Somerset
Gold Brook	Bowman	Oxford
Gold Brook	Chain of Ponds; Kibby	Franklin
Gold Brook	Chase Stream	Somerset
Gold Brook	T5 R6; Appleton Township	Somerset
Nile Brook	Dallas; Rangeley	Franklin
Kibby Stream	Kibby	Franklin
St. Croix River	Baileyville	Washington

The following counties in Maine have each produced some gold: Aroostook, Cumberland, Franklin, Hancock, Kennebec, Knox, Oxford, Penobscot, Somerset, Waldo, and Washington.

There are certainly more areas that likely have gold bearing gravels, and a bit of research will increase your chances of prospecting success.

How to Pan For Gold

When you pan for gold you are going to want a gold pan and some gravel with lead shot or BBs to simulate the gold (flatten the lead shot)

Panning for Gold

Fill a tub with water to do the panning in. Put some gravel in your gold pan, but not too much, start small.

1. Completely lower your pan into a tub of water.
2. Shake your pan in the water to turn your gravel 'soupy'. Don't spill any out yet.
3. Tilt your pan slightly and wash water in and out, gravel should be carried out with the water.
4. After washing out some gravel, level out your pan again and shake it some more.
5. Repeat this process until just the heaviest black sands and gold remain.
6. Swirl water across the black sands and tap the edge of your pan to help separate the gold from sand.

Gold Panning takes practice to get good at but it's a fun and rewarding activity.

The Mechanics of Panning for Gold

When you put some gravel in your pan with water, the gold will be the heaviest thing in the pan. If you are in a stream or river, take your shovel and dig some material from the bottom and place it in your pan. You can use a classifier to sift out the larger material. The objective is to get the gold to the bottom of your pan and wash the sand and gravel out. Place the pan in water get all the material in the pan moving around. There is no right or wrong way to pan. Just do what works the best for you.

Classifier

To remove the sand and gravel, hold both sides of the pan and move it from side to side quickly to loosen the sand and allow the gold to settle to the bottom of the pan. This is called stratification.

To get the sand and gravel out move the pan front to back bringing water into the pan on the forward motion, and floating the lighter materials off on the backward motion. Let the water wash only the top layer of sand out of the pan keeping the material on the bottom motionless.

Steepen the angle each time you shake to bring additional material to the top to wash off. REMEMBER to stratify Use a side to side motion (Stratify) twice as much as front to back (wash). Gold will begin to show as you wash the black sand off of it. Remember the gold is heavy. It will be under all of the black sand on the very bottom of the pan. If you shook and washed correctly it will stay in the pan. Tap the 12:00 o'clock (top) of the pan with your thumb to make the gold jump farther into the side.

As with most everything – Practice makes Perfect – Good Luck

Mineral & Gem Collecting Places

Mining Locations

There are several mining locations between Bethel and South Paris:

- Bethel Outdoor Adventure,
- Songo Pond,
- Western Maine Mineral,
- Creaser Jewelers,
- Perham's of West Paris, and
- Kings' Hill Inn.

These mining locations are very similar and may be the best bet for finding gems such as tourmaline, quartz, rose quartz, and crystal. Mining locations in the Bethel area are centered on Mt. Mica. Unless attending a workshop through Bethel Outdoor Adventure or Western Maine Mineral, mineral. A hammer, shovel, pan, and chisel are helpful tools when sorting through rocks.

Several other mining locations are scattered throughout Maine including Coos Canyon Rock and Gift, Hermit Island, Grafton Notch State Park, Auburn Recreation Parks Department, and the Desert of Maine. Coos Canyon, located on the Swift River in Byron, ME has some gold pockets scattered throughout the river, but is more of a swimming and camping site than a mining hot spot.

Hermit Island has a similar appeal, but is located on the ocean instead of a river. Hermit Island holds some promise of crystal discoveries and mica scatters the beaches at low tide. Both Coos Canyon and Hermit Island are relaxing locations that are perfect for those looking to camp for a weekend near water and possibly find some gold or gems.

Mt. Appetite in Auburn, ME is home to several types of crystals, including green and pink tourmaline, and transparent smoky quartz.

Rangeley Area Gold and Platinum

Northwest of **Byron** is the **Rangeley lake chain**, a popular vacation area in the northeast. In **Nile Brook**, not far from the village of **Rangeley**, both **platinum and gold** have been found. All of the

Gold found in streams like this one

streams flowing into the chain of lakes contain the precious metal, and in a few a numbers of freshwater pearls have been found.

But it is the area extending from the village of **Eustis** southward to **Lake Parmachenne** that causes the excitement among those who search for **gold**. It is generally believed that the mother lode is somewhere in this general area. **Kibbey Brook**, which flows past the village, has produced some outstanding **crystals**, as has the **Magalloway River**, southwest of the town. Trappers often find traces of **gold** while running their lines.

Remember that you're in a region that even prominent scientists believe harbors a fabulous mother lode. There is nothing mythological about the **gold of Maine**.

Verona Island's Gold Mine

There is a real **gold mine** on **Verona Island**. The "Mispickle Mine" actually is not the cave like mine we usually think of as a gold mine but rather a shaft or hole drilled into the ground.

Mispickle is a word of German origin referring to the iron arsenic sulfide Arsenopyrite which is often associated with significant amounts of **gold.**

Gold mining at the "mine" was suspended in the 1940's and converted to mining of the arsenic for use in producing ammunition in support of the war effort.

If you visit **Fort Knox**, just over the "**Narrows Bridge**" from **Verona Island** and overlooking the town of Bucksport, look at the indigenous stones there.

Arsenopyrite

Some will be very dark and heavier than usual stones and may have lighter colored veins in them.

Don't use them to ring your campfire as they have been known to "explode." My wife still bears the scars from our "exploding" Verona Island shore side campfire years ago.

More Lost Treasures

One of Maine's little-known treasures concerns Jim Dolliver, a wealthy sawmill owner who secreted over **$10,000 in gold** for safekeeping between **The Forks, now Manchester, and Murphys**. He had previously made an overland journey to Montral, where had converted his notes, checks, shares, and bonds into **gold sovereigns**. He liked the feel of **gold** rather than paper. This occurred during the 1890s.

During his journey home on the old French trail, Dolliver saw some men following him. Were they going to rob him? Would they kill him? As Jim tore through the dense woods to evade the real, or imagined, robbers, he went completely insane from fear after hiding his money in an old stump.

Relatives later stated that Dolliver died battling imaginary thieves. These same relatives offered three-quarters of the money to whomever should find it, and they spent $3,000 in efforts to discover its whereabouts, to no avail. As far as is known, this cache has never been found.

Moved into Cave to Avoid Neighbors

The little town of **Liberty**, **Waldo County**, also boasts of a **lost treasure of $70,000 in gold coins**. This trove belonged to Timothy Barrett, who lived there in the early 1700s.

Folks noticed that Barrett always seemed to have an inexhaustible supply of money, although he never worked. Was he a retired pirate?

Cave in the woods

That explanation seemed to satisfy his neighbors. In time, the old fellow became vexed with people always asking him about the source of his wealth, so he moved across nearby **George's Stream** and dug a cave for a home. He cultivated a small garden for his simple needs.

When old Barrett finally died, villagers began a great search for his fortune. A couple of fellows dug up an iron kettle near the cave. It was filled with ancient **French coins**. However, this was believed to have been only a small part of the main cache, which is still safe in the ground near **George's Stream**.

Benedict Arnold's Gold

Not even contemporaries of **Benedict Arnold** knew how much was in the lost **chest of gold**. Supposedly lost beneath one of the falls of the **Chaudire River**, on the abortive march against the walls of Quebec, the loot has never been found. During Arnold's famous court martial in Philadelphia, he was asked to account for the money, and while the one-day traitor did produce sketchy records accounting for $5,000, the remainder was **lost in the forest wilderness of Maine**, he claimed.

Chests under water

While no one is certain, the chest and the gold are supposed to be somewhere **north of the modern village of Stratton on the Dead River**, although many claim it was the **Chaudire River**.

Treasure Protected by Spirits

Monhegan Island, off the Maine coast, contains a cave, opening to the sea, where it was whispered that treasure had been stored in care of spirits. Searchers found within it a heavy chest, which they were about to lift when one of the party—contrary to orders—spoke.

The spell was broken, for the watchful spirits heard and snatched away the treasure.

Shipwrecks

South Coast to Casco Bay

The Isles of Shoals Area

The Isles of Shoals consist of nine islands, five located in Maine and four in New Hampshire. We begin our survey of ships wrecked along Maine's rocky shores here.

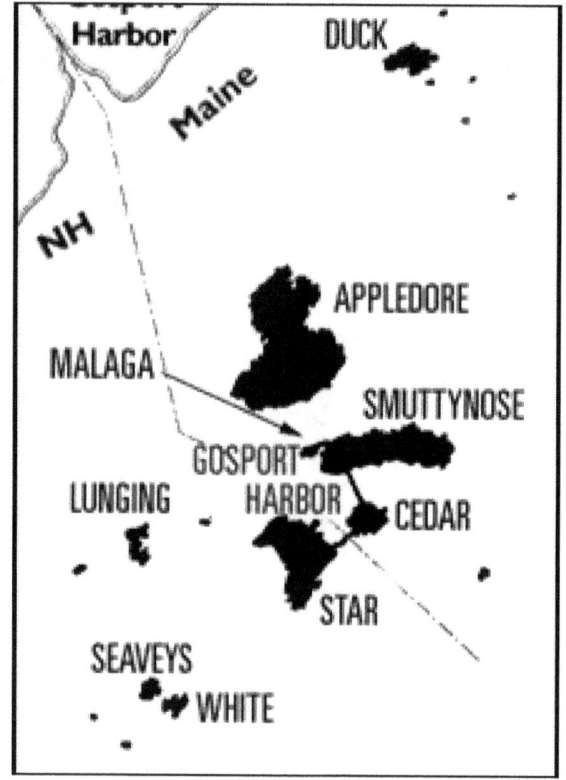

Map provided by SeacoastNH.com

There have been nearly twenty shipwrecks on the rocky shoals with the wreck of the Spanish frigate "Sagunto" in 1813 being the first to be recorded. Many other ships with unknown names have been lost here as well.

Some of the Known Isles of Shoals Shipwrecks

Sagunto, Frigate – 1/14/1813
Belle – 8/7/1877
Turkish Empire, 3/7/1879
Samuel J Goucher Schooner – 11/12/1911
Pearl Nelson, Schooner 8/29/1914
Hume. – 3/21/1916
Florida, Cruiser – 10/3/1916
Nanticoke, Schooner – 5/15/1919
USCG Leader -4/2/1920
USS 0-9, Submarine – 6/21/1941
William H Machen, Freighter – 3/2/1943

USS 0-9 (SS70)

This submarine sank while on trial run performing a test dive off the Isles of Shoals. Her hull was crushed killing the entire crew of thirty three men.

She was 172' long and built in 1918 at the Quincy Shipyard in Massachusetts.

She lies on the bottom at a depth of 430 feet.

USS O-9 (SS 70)

South Coast to Casco Bay

1710 (December 11) *Nottingham*, British Galley – **off Boon Island**

1756 (October 5) *Argo*, Privateer

1760 *Friendly Adventure* - **off Kittery**

1776 Unidentified off Wells Beach circa

1777 (December 17) *Resolution* – **off Kittery**

1806 - The Schooner *Charles* going from Boston to Portland with 25 passengers, wrecked on Little Island. The bodies were found on **Crescent Beach**

Bulwark fires on Biddeford Pool

1807 *Jonathan Sawyer*, Schooner – near **Cape Porpoise**

1814 - English Frigate *Bulwark* attacked **Biddeford Pool**. The *Harmoine*, *Catherine* and *Equator* were sunk. One ship in the stocks (unknown name) was burned and one ship, the *Victory*, was stolen for ransom of $6,000.

1820 (January 1) *Charles H Hickey*, Schooner – near **Cape Porpoise**

1823 (January 12) *Robert W* – **off York**

1831 (April 2) Schooner, *Nellie A Walker* off **Boon Island**

1836 (May 31) *Tom Thumb* - near **Boon Island**

1836 (May 31) *New England* – near **Boon Island**

1840 (November) - *William and Harris* wrecks near **Negro island**, in route from New York to Maine

1851 (April) - *Augusta* wrecks near **Wood Island**

1854 (December 22) *Maria*, - near **Cape Porpoise**

1855 (February) *Three Sisters*, Schooner – near **Wells**

1855 (December 1) *Hope* – near **Wells**

1856 (May) *Mercard*, - near **Cape Porpoise**

1856 (December 14) - *American Schooner, Washington* wrecked west of **Wood Island**

1857 - *Admiral*, Schooner, near Ft Constitution, New Castle, NH and **Kittery**

1860 (November) - Schooner *Hiawatha* wrecked in the vicinity of **Wood Island.**

1865 – (March 16) *Edyth Ann*, Schooner – **Washburn Ledge**

1867 (September) - American Schooner *Game Cock* holed on a rock and run into the beach with cargo of fish

1869 (October) - American Schooner *Nellie Grant* sank near **Biddeford Pool**

1869 (December) - *Eva* wrecked near **Old Orchard Beach.**

1872 (Dec. 24th) - The American Schooner *Intrepid* with 15 tons of iron struck the outer reef of **Wood Island.** Christmas morning the captain and crew made their way to the Lighthouse. The captain's wife had small pox and was cared for by the keeper's family

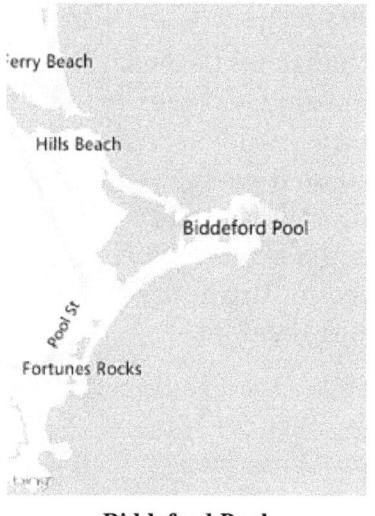

Biddeford Pool

1872 (Dec. 24th) - The American Schooner *Smith Tuttle* of Wiscassett, went ashore at **Wood Island**, was off with no injuries.

1872 (Dec. 24th) - The ship *Virginia* went onto **Wood Island**. Came off the same day and went into the **Pool**

1874 (March) - The *George Osborn* wrecks on **Negro Ledge**

1876 (July 6) *Challenge* – near **Wells**

1877 (August 13) *Belle* - near **Kittery**

1883 (July) C W *Loche,* - near **Cape Porpoise**

1883 - The *Alice G. Norwood* wrecked on north side of **Stage Island** on September 29th. All survived.

1886 (March) - The *Alice T. Bailey* wrecked near the Life Station (on Ocean Ave., **Biddeford Pool**, all of the crew survived.

1886 (November) - *Clear the Track* wrecked on **Wood Island**, all crew rescued, cargo of bricks lost, these bricks may have been made in Biddeford.

1887 (November) - American Schooner *George and Albert* wrecked near **Wood Island.**

1887 - The Schooner *Western Light* was wrecked with a cargo of household items. Captain Gear was in charge. All was lost and as it washed ashore but items were picked up and used by **Biddeford Pool** residents.

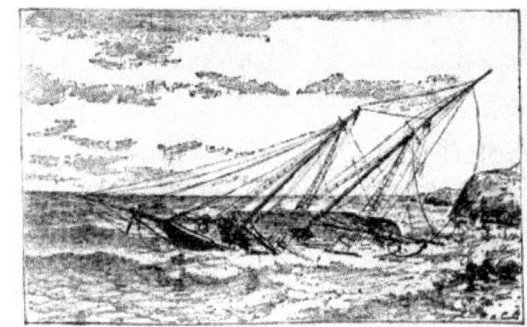

Schooner on the rocks

1887 - One evening the schooner *Cora Van Gilder* ran aground on rocks near **Fletchers Neck (now Biddeford Pool).**

As the Captain waited for the tide to free his ship naturally, some residents of the Pool rowed out to see if they could help. Captain Gear declined their help

He indicated that his wife was sick with small pox. Some men scurried away but three remained and took the sick woman to a building on **Wood Island**. The keeper and family took care of the woman until a doctor arrived. Captain Gear's wife recovered and no one else became ill.

1888 (December) - *George Cushing* wrecked on **Richmond Island.**

1889 (November 27) Schooner, *City of Ellsworth* off **Boon Island**

1891 (April 9) *Nellie J Day*, Schooner – near **Boon Island**

1891 (December 15) *Dolphin,* Schooner – near **Boon Island**

1892 (April) - *The Index* wrecked on **Stage Island**

1896 (February) - The *Majestic* wrecked on **Beach Island off the Pool.**

1897 (August) - The 3 masted American Coastal Schooner, *Howard W. Middleton*, on her way to Portland with a cargo of coal struck ledge in **Saco Bay**.

1898 (June) - The schooner *Grecian Bend* wrecked off of **Old Orchard Beach**. Debris from the wreck took out part of the **Old Orchard Beach pier**.

1898 (November) - American Schooner *Queen of the West* wrecked near **Fletchers Neck** in route from Boston to Bangor.

Boon Island Lighthouse

1900 (December) - Two masted Schooner *Fannie & Edith*, wrecked in **Saco Bay**

1900 (December) - The *R.P. Chase* wrecked at the **Pool in the Gut.**

1900 (December) The *Thomas B. Reed* wrecked at the **Pool in the Gut.**

1903 (June) - Five Masted Schooner *Washington B. Thomas*, bound from Virginia to Portland with cargo of 4,226 tons of coal, wrecked on reefs of **Stratton Island, Saco Bay.**

1903 (June) – Ship, name unknown, wrecked on **Stratton Island, Saco Bay.**

1903- The US Government *Steam Launch 284* wrecked on **Little Beach Island of South Point, Biddeford Pool.**

1905 - Three schooners from St. John carrying cordwood to Boston were lost on their return trip (lacking ballast) off **Wood Island**

1905 - The *Annie L. Wilder* caught fire and burned carrying a load of lime. The entire harbor area around **Biddeford Pool** was aglow.

1906 (April 10) *Rising Star*, - near **Wells**

1906 (November) - American Schooner *Marshall Perrin* wrecked on **Wood Island**. Captain and cook lost their lives.

1907 (October 9) *R P Chase*, near **Cape Porpoise**

1907 (November) - The *Susan Stetson* loaded with coal sank off of **Biddeford Pool**, bound from New Jersey to Camden, Maine.

1907 (November 16) *Marshall Ferris*, Schooner –near **Wells**

1907 (November) - The *Jonathan Sawyer* wrecked off **Cape Porpoise** with load of coal intended for the Pepperell Manufacturing Company. She had previously wrecked on the rocks of Martha's Vineyard the same trip but was refloated.

1909 (July) – The gas powered launch *Item* capsized near **Wood Island**. 31 passengers were aboard. Two women drowned. Help came from President Taft's yacht *Sylph*.

President Taft's Yacht *Sylph*

1909 (October) - Canadian Schooner *Valetta* wrecked on **Wood Island**. She had a load of wood and was coming from St. Johns New Brunswick bound for Boston. She struck **Dansbury Ledge.**

1911 (December 11) *Ella* May, - 12/11/1911 of **Cape Porpoise**

1912 (February 26) *Mildred V Numan*, Schooner – near **Cape Porpoise**

1912 (March 7) *Jessie Lane* – near **Wells**

1914 (January 2) *Mary Augusta,* - near **Wells**

1916 (April) *Silver Spray* – **near Wells**

1917 (January) - American Schooner *Roger Drury* foundered near **Biddeford Pool.**

1917 (March) - The *Wabash* wrecks on **Richmond Island.**

1917 (May) - American Gas Screw *Rara Avis* crushed near **Biddeford Pool.**

1917 (October 14) *E McNichol,* Schooner – near **Boon Island**

1918 (January 22) *Robert and Richard* – near **Boon Island**

1919 (November 29) *A F Kindberg* – near **Wells**

1920 (January 1) *Mary E Olys*, Schooner – **Cape Porpoise**

1920 (January 1) *Charles H. Trickey,* Schooner – **Cape Porpoise**

The Mary Olys and Charles H Trickey aground at the entrance to Cape Porpoise Harbor

1920 (October) - American Schooner "Fred Tyler" blown onto **Big Beach at the Pool.** She was bound west with full cargo of lumber.

1921 (January 2) *Wandby, British Steamer* - near **Wells**

1923 (January 12) *Robert H*, near **Cape Porpoise**

1923 (April 15) - American Screw *Anahuac* stranded on rocks near **Fortunes Rocks**

1925 (August) - *Southward lll* wrecks on **Richmond Island.**

1925 (September 25) *Livelyhood* – near **Wells**

1925 (October) - American Schooner *C.N. Gilmore* goes ashore on **Wood Island.**

1925 (December 27) *Edward J. Lawrence* 320' 6 masted Schooner - **Portland Harbor**, between Diamond Island and Fort Gorges

1931 (March 2) - Schooner *Fleetwing*, on **Biddeford Pool**

1931 (August 30) – Schooner *St John*, off **Cape Porpoise**

1934 - The freighter *Sagamore* struck Corwin's Ledge off Prout's Neck, **Saco Bay**. She was bound from Portland to New York

1936 (March 21) *Hume* - off **Kittery**

1937 (July 6) *Florence,* - near **Cape Porpoise**

1938 (January 12) - *Roger Drury*, Schooner on **Biddeford Pool**

1941 (June 21) *USS 0-9*, Submarine – off **Isles of Shoals**

1942 (May 17) *Skottland*, Cargo ship – torpedoed off **Kittery** by German submarine *U-588*

1942 (October 24) - *Dominion Mahyd*, Trawler – at sea off **York beach**

1944 (March 11) *Empire Knight*. Freighter – near **Boon Island**

1945 (April 23) *USS PC- 36, Submarine* – near **Wells**

2000 (February 20) *Jessica Ann* – near **Wells**

Details and Stories of a Few of the Wrecks

Nottingham Galley - 1710

Perhaps the most famous shipwreck was that of the shipwreck the British merchant ship, *Nottingham Galley* on December 11, 1710. All fourteen crewmen aboard survived the initial wreck, however two died from their injuries and another two drowned attempting to reach the mainland on an improvised raft.

The remaining ten crewmen managed to stay alive despite winter conditions with no food and no firewood for twenty four days, until finally rescued.

Cannibalism

They resorted to cannibalism which gave the incident a notoriety that it retains even today. It is said that after this disaster, local fishermen began leaving barrels of provisions on Boon Island in case of future wrecks. The harrowing story was fictionalized by Kenneth Roberts in his 1956 novel *Boon Island*.

Ghosts of the Wreck "Sagunto"

Are ancient Spanish sailors haunting Smuttynose?

Are 14 shipwrecked Spanish sailors from the Spanish frigate *Sagunto* really buried on Smuttynose Island? Is it their ghosts that have been alarming visitors to Smuttynose, on the Isles of Shoals, for centuries?

Legend has it that the fourteen sailors were buried on the rocky island in January of 1813 are haunting the island today.

A Spanish Frigate of the era

Two poets, James Kennard Jr. and Celia Thaxter, have turned the legend into poetry. Their poems record the events that transpired and lament, along with the wives and girl friends, the loss of the dead sailors.

Thaxter wrote:

> *Spanish women, over the far seas,*
> *Could I but show you where your dead repose!*
> *Could I send tidings on this northern breeze*
> *That strong and steady blows!*

Kennard wrote:

> *No mourners stood around their graves,*
> *No friends above them wept ;*
> *A hasty prayer was uttered there, --*
> *Unknown, unknelled, they slept.*

Edyth Ann - 1865

Heroic Lighthouse Keeper

Ebenezer (Eben) Emerson was appointed keeper of the Wood Island Lighthouse by President Lincoln. He was destined to become a hero.

At 1:00 AM on March 16, 1865, Emerson heard the cries from the people aboard the brig *Edyth Ann* of Nova Scotia. She was loaded with molasses and sugar from Puerto Rico bound for Portland, Maine. She had run aground on **Washburn Ledge** off **Wood Island Lighthouse**.

Wood Island Lighthouse

Through his single handed heroics, Emerson was able to save the entire crew.

On June, 1865, the Canadian (British at the time) government cited Keeper Emerson's heroism and awarded him a pair of brass binoculars in a rosewood box with a plaque honoring his heroic efforts

The brass plaque on the top of the box reads:

> *"Presented by the British Government to Mr. Eben Emerson, Lighthouse Keeper, Wood Island in recognition of his humane services to the crew of the Edyth Ann of Digby, Nova Scotia on 16th March, 1865."*

Binoculars and Plaque

Samuel J Goucher - 1911

She was a 5-masted schooner 282' long built in 1904 at Camden, ME. She ran aground in a fog on November 16, 1911 off **Duck Island,** Isles of Shoals.

Samuel J. Goucher
Painting by Samuel Badger

Pearl Nelson - 1914

On August 29th, 1914, the schooner Pearl Nelson on voyage from Dennysville, Me. to Mystic, Conn. with a cargo of lumber, sprang a leak during a North East gale and capsized off the Isles of Shoals.

The captain and the cook drowned attempting to swim ashore. The other three crew members lashed themselves to the masts until the ship ran aground. There they were able to leap into the surf and struggle ashore and safety. The ship was a total loss.

USCG Leader – 1919

Originally named "Admiral" she was a wooden-hulled motorboat built in Boothbay, Maine, in 1913. The US Navy acquired the "Admiral" in May of 1917 for patrol duty and was placed in commission on May 31, 1917.

The Navy transferred "Admiral" to the Coast Guard on April 21, 1919, *and* that June, stationed at Portsmouth, NH.

She was renamed *Leader* on December, 16 1919 by the Coast Guard. However, she did not serve long for on April 2, 1920, her gasoline tank exploded, and the resultant fire totally destroyed the boat.

USCG Leader

Twin Wrecks at Cape Porpoise
Two ships – One storm - 1920

January 1, 1920 these two ships were wrecked during the same storm, New Years eve 1920 at **Cape Porpoise**, ME - at harbor entrance, across channel from lighthouse.

The *Charles H Tuckey* came in on the wrong side of the channel buoy and ran aground on the ledge.

Later the *Mary F Olys* attempted to pass the grounded *Tuckey* and crashed heavily into the ledge. She broke into

Charles H. Trickey **(left) and** *Mary E. Olys*

pieces within five minutes of running aground; the *Tuckey* was able to be refloated and survived to sail yet another day.

The Wandby – 1921

Assumed lost – reappears - shipwrecked

She was thought to be lost while on a voyage the White Sea. Upon return the captain was surprised to learn that the insurance companies had paid off on the vessel as a total loss.

Additionally, funeral services had been held for every member of the crew, it being assumed they were lost at sea, and they were "buried" and mourned by their families and friends.

It was against this backdrop that the Wandby sailed to America. While sailing off the Maine coast it is believed that, the captain mistook Wood Island Light for a lighthouse much further south. She ran aground while in a fog near Walker's Point, Kennebunkport. Wreck is located just off shore.

The Wandby on the rocks

USS Squalus (SS-192) - 1939

Sank on first cruise

The Squalus was built at Portsmouth Naval Shipyard in Portsmouth, NH in 1938. She was carrying a crew of fifty nine men when she sank during sea trials on May 23, 1939.

Thirty three crewmen were rescued, twenty six perished in the tragedy.

Squalus was raised from a depth of two hundred forty feet, refitted and re-commissioned as *USS Sailfish*

Squalus with rescue bell on deck

USS 0-9 (SS70) - 1941

Sank while on a test dive

This submarine sank while on trial run performing a test dive off the Isles of Shoals. Her hull was crushed killing the entire crew of thirty three men.

She was 172' long and built in 1918 at the Quincy Shipyard in Massachusetts.

She lies on the bottom at a depth of 430 feet.

USS O-9 (SS 70)

The Skottland - 1942

Victim of the German Submarine U-588

Cargo ship similar to the *Skottland*

On May 17, 1942, the unescorted Skottland was torpedoed on the port side by the German submarine U-588 miles off the **Kittery** shore. Two torpedoes hit the ship. The explosions stopped the engines and the ship lost all power.

Lifeboats were launched with great difficulty because of the heavy list to port. Several of the crew later transferred onto two rafts that floated free after the ship sank.

Survivors were picked up by a Canadian lobster boat after being spotted by a Canadian aircraft and taken to Boston where they were treated.

Torpedoed by German Sub

William H. Machen - 1943
Freighter - 1943

The freighter *William H Machen* sank after a collision with with steamship *Maid of Stirling* east of White Island, Isles of Shoals March 2nd, 1943. The freighter lies three hundred feet deep; the *Maid of Stirling* was able to sail away under her own steam.

Maid of Stirling sails away

Empire Knight, Freighter - 1944

On February 1944, the *Empire Knight*, a 428-foot British freight ship, ran aground at Boon Island and later broke into two sections. The stern section, which included the ship's cargo holds, sank in approximately 260 feet of water, one and one half miles from the Island.

In August 1990, the United States Coast Guard became aware of the existence of a plan of stowage dating from 1944 for the ship indicating that 221 flasks of mercury may have been loaded onto the vessel. Investigation revealed that such flasks had been placed on the ship but had since deteriorated, releasing the mercury. An estimated 16,000 pounds of mercury remain unrecovered and is believed to have settled in the low point of the cargo hold.

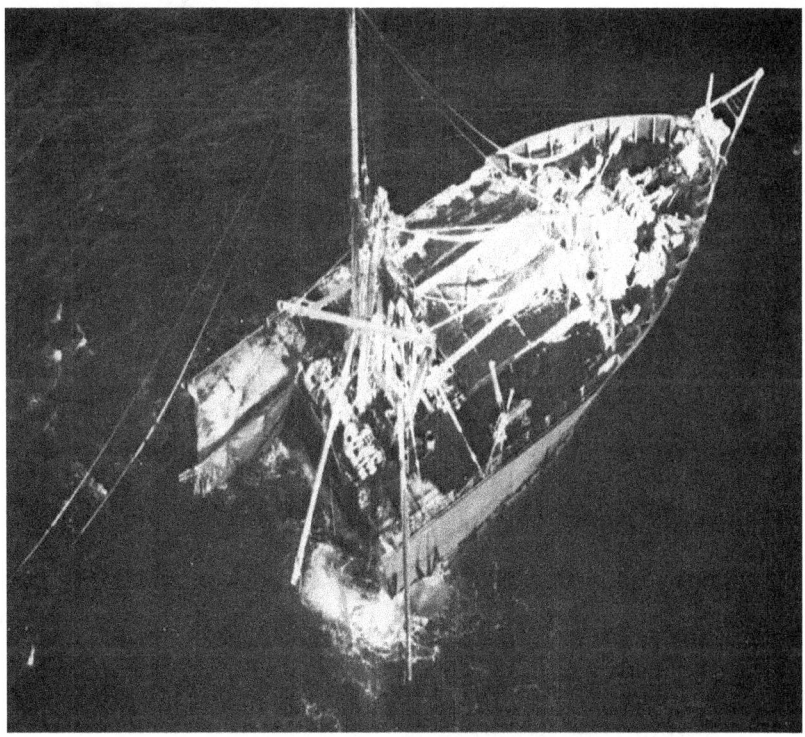

Bow section of the *Empire Knight* on Boon Island Ledge

USS *Eagle 56* (PE-56) - 1945

It took 55 years to realize the ship had been torpedoed by a German submarine

The Eagle was a United States Navy World War I era patrol boat that remained in service through World War II. On 23 April 1945, while towing targets for US Navy bomber exercises off **Portland**, the ship suffered a massive explosion.

Although *Eagle 56* survivors stated they had spotted a submarine during the sinking, the official Navy Investigation declared it lost due to a boiler explosion.

U.S. Navy photo

Through the work of a dedicated researcher and the Naval Historical Center's senior archivist the Navy changed this to a combat loss in 2002.

In fact, *Eagle 56* had been sunk by the German submarine *U-853*. Only 13 of the 67 crew survived.

The ship was one of 60 Eagle Boats built by automaker Henry Ford for World War I. None of them were completed in time to see service in that war due to the Armistice, November 11, 1918.

The Navy had decommissioned all but eight of the sixty before the outbreak of World War II. The term Eagle Boat came from a 1917 editorial in the Washington Post that called for an "eagle to scour the seas and pounce upon and destroy every German submarine."

The Gruesome Tale of a Christmas Day Shipwreck

This is a graphic account of the Christmas Day storm in 1778 that took place in Plymouth Harbor in Massachusetts, of which present day Maine was a part at the time.

This story is a good representation of the horrors that have been repeated time and again in violent storms all along the rocky coast of Maine.

Wreck of the Arnold

It was Christmas 1778, and snow was falling upon Boston Harbor. The brigantine General Arnold, named for the gallant hero of Quebec, was at anchor off Nantasket Road. In the early dawn, she set sail for the Carolinas, alongside the privateer Revenge (the Revenge is one of the ships lost in the Battle for New Ireland which we chronicle in a later chapter).

The Brigantine General Arnold

The Arnold carried 21 guns, a detachment of Marines, and a cargo of military supplies for the American troops who were attempting to stop the British from cutting off the South from the Northern colonies. Her commander was Captain James Magee, an Irish born American patriot, who was looking forward to meeting up with the British, his lieflong enemy. Before the day was over, however, he would lose his ship to a greater enemy, the enraged sea.

Of the 105 men and boys who sailed with him, 81 would die a horrible death, and the others, all but himself, would be crippled for life. Under full sail, the privateers headed across Massachusetts Bay toward the open sea. The wind picked up, the snow fell harder, and soon they were in the midst of a

Nor'East blizzard. Captain Barrows of the Revenge decided to ride out the storm off Cape Cod. Magee felt that his ship could weather the storm better in Plymouth Harbor behind Gurnet Point. But, the Arnold's anchor wouldn't hold, and she began to drift into the long harbor.

Magee had his men dismount 16 of the deck cannons and store them below to add weight to the hull and give the vessel stability. Her sails were furled and to the topmost struck, but nothing seemed to stop The Arnold's dragging anchor. Huge waves broke over the bow and quickly turned to ice.

The anchor cable broke and the Arnold sailed backwards into the harbor, bumped over a sand bar, and scraped to a sudden stop on top of shallow water sand flat, only a mile from shore.

At first, Magee and his men thought they could lighten the vessel and slide her over the flat to shore. With axes, they cut down her masts, but the heavy hull was already sinking into the sand, cracking her boards and leaking salt water into her hold. Icy waves washed over her main deck and the captain later reported "The quarter deck was the only place that could afford the most distant prospect of safety." Magee went on to say "Within a few hours, presented a scene that would shock the least delicate humanity. Some of my people were stifled to death with the snow, others perished with the extremity of the cold, and a few were washed off the deck and drowned."

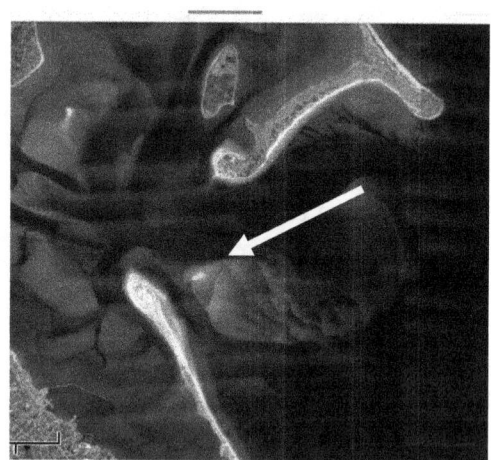

Arrow points to the resting place of the Brigantine General Arnold outside Plymouth Harbor

There were a few bottles and casks of wine and brandy in the cargo. Some of the crew members ventured below into the half flooded hold to drown themselves in liquid warmth. Some were drunk before Captain Magee realized they had broken into the stores. He pleaded with them to pour the brandy into their shoes to prevent frostbite, instead of drinking it. Some obeyed, but those who did not were dead by the next morning. Those huddled together on the quarterdeck, their clothes first drenched then frozen to their bodies, covered themselves with the sails for protection from the salt spray and the snow. By the morning of the 26th, thirty of them were frozen to death. The blizzard continued. Magee could see but a shadow of land through the falling snow, so he fired his signal gun in hopes of getting the attention of the people of the town. Three crewmen managed to launch the privateers long boat into the wild sea, then started rowing to shore, but they were lost sight of and never heard from again.

Late in the afternoon when there was a short break in the storm, the people of Plymouth sent dories out from shore, however, none of them could make it to the stranded vessel. They decided that the only way to the Arnold was to build a causeway of ice and snow one mile long out to the sand flat. Working throughout the night, through the next day and night, the people of Plymouth accomplished what seemed impossible - they built a road out to the distressed privatee.

Rescue attempt

Meanwhile the shipwreck victims spent a second and third night on the quarter-deck in sub-freezing temperatures. The living feared going to sleep, knowing that if they did, they probably would not wake up again. In an attempt to block out wind and waves, they piled the dead bodies of their comrades around them. The Arnold sank deeper into the sand, knee deep water now covering the main deck. In an effort to keep his remaining crewmen and Marines alive, Captain Magee requested, then demanded, that the men keep walking around and exercising on the little deck in order to maintain their circulation.

He was especially anxious about two boys aboard: Connie Marchang, age 10 and Barney Downs, age 15. Magee prodded them to walk in place even though they were both so exhausted and frozen they could hardly stand. He urged them over and over agin not to give up. Marchant later said, "I ascribe my preservation mainly to the reiterated efforts of Captain Magee."

On Monday morning, December 28th when the causeway was completed, the people of Plymouth passed over the ice to the wreck. "It was a scene unutterably awful and distressing, writes Plymouth's Doctor Thatcher. "The ship was sunk ten feet in the sand; the waves had been for about thirty six hours sweeping the main deck, and even here they were obliged to pile together dead bodies to make room for the living. Seventy dead bodies, frozen in to all imaginable postures, were strewn over the deck, or attached to shrouds and spars; about thirty exhibited signs of life, but were unconscious whether in life or death. The bodies remained in the posture in which they died, the features dreadfully distorted. Some were erect, some bending forward, some sitting with the head resting on the knees, and some with both arms extended, clinging to spars or some part of the vessel."

Sleds and slabs of wood were used to carry the survivors and the stiffened corpses over the ice road to shore. The dead were piled in the Plymouth Courthouse, the living brought to local homes to spend agonizing hours thawing out.

Magee skippered merchant ships out of Salem for the remainder of his life, including the famous *Astrea* that opened American trade with China. Whenever in home port at Christmas, Magee called for a reunion of the 24 Arnold survivors, assisting any who were destitute with a gift from his own wages. At his request, when he died, he was buried with the Arnold crew at Burial Hill, Plymouth, MA..

Author unknown

Cape Elizabeth to Casco Bay

1710 (December 11) *Nottingham,* British Galley - Struck rocks and sank at **Boon Island**, off **York** — 4 fatalities, 10 survivors, Crew members were marooned on Boon Island for 28 days before being rescued.

1758 *Pheonix* — **Casco Bay**

1790 *Nancy*, Brig- Privateer — scuttled to avoid capture by the British, off **Cape Elizabeth**, approximately 150' north of **Portland Head lighthouse.**

1803 (July 12) *Charles,* Schooner on **Richmond Island**

1807 *Charles,* Schooner — **Near Portland Light**

1853 (February 25) *Nellie Bowers,* near **Portland**

1854 (December 18) *Mary,* Schooner — **Near Portland Light**

Portland Head Lighthouse

1855 (March) *Foster,* Brig — **Near Portland Light**

1857 (March) *Hualco* near **Monhegan Island**

1863 (February 22) The Steamship *Bohemian* bound from Liverpool to Portland with 218 passengers wrecked off **Cape Elizabeth, Saco Bay**.

1865 (June 6) *Potomac,* Steamer — **off Cape Elizabeth**

1869 (September 8) *Helen Eliza,* Fishing Schooner - Ran on rocks and broke up, eleven fatalities - Southeast side of **Peak's Island, Casco Bay**

1872 (May 28) *Emperor,* Sidewheel Steamer - Eastern Ledge, off **Seal Island**

Emperor ran aground in a fog on a trip from Yarmouth (NS) to Portland After the vessel struck, about 80 passengers and crew members took to life boats and landed safely several hours later on **Matinicus Rock.** The vessel was later removed from the ledge and taken to the mainland for salvage.

1878 (January 11) *Ulysses,* Side-wheel Steamer - Broke from moorings in gale at night, ran onto rocks and broke up - **Rockland Harbor**

1883 (December 27) *Gen. W Cushing,* Schooner on **Richmond Island**

1885 (March 13) *Solon,* Schooner – **Portland** area

1885 (May) *Radius,* Brig - **Portland** area

1885 (July 5) *Amethyst,* Schooner - **Portland** area

1885 (October 12) *Julia and Martha,* Schooner – **Portland** area

1886 (December 25) *Anne C Maguire,* Schooner – on **Portland Head Lighthouse**

1886 (February 10) *Cambridge,* Side-wheeler – **Port Clyde**

1886 (March 31) *David Nicholls,* Bark – **Portland** area

Anne C Mcquire

1887 (July 6) *Hudson,* Schooner – **Portland** area

1897 (December 14) *Susan P Thurlow* - **Portland** area

1889 (October 1) *S Hammond,* Schooner – **Portland** area

1890 (May 9) *Gertrude,* Schooner – **Portland** area

1890 (January 24) *Fairfield,* Schooner – off **Small Point, Casco Bay**

1890 (October 7) *T B Harris*, Schooner, - **Portland** area

1891 (January 13) *Ada Barker*, Schooner – **Portland** area

1891 (March 4) *Helen*, Schooner - **off Cape Elizabeth**

1897 (December 14) *Susan P. Thurlow*, 126' Three Masted Schooner –Hit a ledge during a gale off south end of **Cushing's Island, Casco Bay**, six drowned – one survived

1903 (June 12) 2 months after being launched -*Washington B. Thomas*, 5 Masted Schooner – Captain's wife drowned - **Stratton Island, Saco Bay**

1904 *Fortune*, Schooner - near **Cape Elizabeth**

1906 (April 10) *Sally B*, Schooner - **Casco Bay**

1907 (January 7) *Mary E. Oyls*, Schooner – **Goat Island**

Washington B Thomas

1907 (January 22) *Fisher*man, Schooner - **off Cape Elizabeth**

1907 (November 28) *Kanawha*, Steamer -

1908 (September 27) *Race Horse*, Schooner - **Casco Bay**

1910 (March 7) *Manhattan*, Steamer – **Portland** area

1910 (June 29) *Young Brothers*, Schooner on **Richmond Island**

1910 (November 18) *John Calwellader*, Schooner - **off Cape Elizabeth**

1912 (January 8) *Empress*, Schooner - **off Cape Elizabeth**

1912 (June 30) *Sallie L'Orr*, Schooner, - **Portland** area

1913 (September 9) *Abdon Keene*, Schooner – near **Orr's Island**

1914 (October 27) *Chandler R*, Cargo Ship – **Casco Bay**

1915 (December 9) *Flora D Thompson*, Sloop – near **Sequin Island Lighthouse**

1915 (December 26) *William L Elkins*, Schooner - **off Cape Elizabeth**

1916 (September 5) *Donna T Bridges*, Schooner - **Casco Bay**

1916 (September 23) *Bay State*, Sternwheeler – **Near Portland Light**

1917 (March 17) *Cumberland, Tug* - Penobscot Bay, Green Island, at the entrance to **Vinalhaven Harbor**

1917 (March 17) *Harry W Hayes*, Schooner - **Portland** area

1918 (June 1) *Annie Lee,* Oil Tanker - **Casco Bay**

1918 (June 7) *James Young*, Schooner – **Near Portland Light**

1918 (August 23) *Elk* - near **Monhegan Island**

1918 (October 15) *C and R Tarbox*. Tanker- **Portland** area

Wandby on Walker's Point

1918 (September 5) *Herman F Kimball*, Schooner - off **Cape Elizabeth**

1918 (November 29) Merryconeag, Cargo Ship – off **Orr's Island**

1920 (March 13) *Wabash*, Schooner on **Richmond Island**

1921 (March 9) *Wandby,* British Freighter - **Walker's Point, Kennebunkport**

1921 (July 9) *Odell*, Schooner – **Portland** area

1922 (November 9) *Samuel Hart*, Schooner - **Casco Bay**

1920 (November 21) *Pocasset*, Schooner – off **Cape Elizabeth**

1922 (December 1*) Flora Temple*, Cargo Ship – near **Falmouth**

1923 (April 29) *Francis Goodnow,* Schooner – **on McKinney Point**

1923 (October 14) *Eugenie,* Schooner – off **Small Point, Casco Bay**

1925 (December 27) *Edward J Lawrence,* Schooner – **Portland**

1926 (April 1) *Lillian,* Schooner – near **Falmouth**

1930's *F C Pendleton,* 3-Masted Schooner - **Seal Harbor, Islesboro** Caught fire while anchored

1930's *Gardner G. Deering,* 5 Masted Schooner – 500' off **Smith Cove, West Brooksville,**

Hesper (at left) with Luther Little

1932 *Hesper,* 4-Masted Schooner – an icon for years has finally succumbed to time and tide, no longer visible - **Sheepscot River, Wiscasset**

1934 (January 14) *Sagamore,* Freighter - Struck **Corwin Rock** in a storm - **Prout's Neck, Scarborough**, 300 yards off south end of **Jordan's Beach.**

1934 (March 13) *Bourne,* Barge – **Portland** area

1935 (December 31) *Gov. Douglas,* Tanker – **Portland** area

1942 (May 29) *Benjamin Thompson,* Cargo Ship – off **Small Point, Casco Bay**

1943 (May 5) *Hartwelson,* Cargo Ship - Struck **Bantam Rock** and foundered - 8 miles south of **Boothbay Harbor**

1945 (March 9) *Tyr,* Cargo Ship - 1947 - off **Portland**

1947 (March 3) *Oakley L Alexander,* Steamer - **on McKinney Point**

1992 (January 16) *Harkness,* Tug - near **Matinicus Island** - off **Zephyr Ledges**

1947 (March 11) *Novadoc,* Cargo Ship - Disappeared in gale, entire crew of 24 lost, Last distress call: "Taking on water, 22 miles east of **Portland,** ME"

1950 (July 30) *Charles A Smith*, Cargo Ship – off **Bailey Island**

1959 (September 6) *John M Hathaway*, Tanker – **Portland** area

1963 (November 11) *Higendorf,* Gsw – **Portland** area

1967 (January 24) *Alice M Doherty II*, Tanker – **Near Portland Light**

1963 (July 6) *Andrew J Ward*, Tanker - **Casco Bay**

1967 (January 24) *Alice M Doherty III*, Trawler, off **Cape Elizabeth**

1972 (December 4) *Alton A, Trawler* - off **Cape Elizabeth**

1973 (November 17) J H Deinlein - near **Monhegan Island**

Details and Stories of Wrecks

Cape Elizabeth to Casco Bay

Bohemian, Steamer - 1864

1864 off Cape Elizabeth

On the night of February 22, 1864, the steamer Bohemian was heading to Portland. The first officer had just taken the wheel when the Bohemian struck **Alden's Rock**, near **Cape Elizabeth**, ripping a gash in the hull and flooding the engine room.

The captain headed the vessel toward shore and into Broad Cove, where the disabled steamer could go no further because of the water she had taken on.

The captain ordered the lifeboats deployed. While most lifeboats were able to safely launch, a support pin in lifeboat

Wreck of the Bohemian 1864

number two gave way, spilling passengers into the ocean resulting in most of the casualties

Two hundred and fifty survived with forty two fatalities.

The wreck of the Bohemian was a factor in raising Portland Head Light twenty feet and the installation of a more powerful, second order lens being installed.

Schooner MARY ALICE -1869

Schooner Mary Alice Wrecked.

The Schooner Mary Alice, before reported lost on Trundy's Reef, near Cape Elizabeth, Me., was a schooner of about 90 tons burden and valued at about $5,000. She was engaged in carrying lumber from Lincolnville to New York and returning with coal.

At the time she was wrecked she was making for Portland. About 5 P.M. Saturday she was abreast Cape Elizabeth Light, when the weather shut down thick and it commenced snowing. The captain immediately headed her for Portland harbor, under double reefed mainsail and jib. They saw a light, supposed it was Portland Light, and hauled the vessel to for it. They were deceived by the light, which proved to be one in John Trundy's house, and as soon as they hauled to the vessel struck the reef.

As soon as she struck the crew hauled the jib to weather and payed her off shore, and, after a time, succeeded in working her off, but it was evident that she had stove her port bow when she struck, for she filled and was capsized. At the time she first hit on the rocks it was 7:20 P.M. The crew clung to the vessel, hoping, yet doubting, that succor might come. At 2 o'clock Sunday morning the captain could hold out no longer, being thoroughly exhausted and almost frozen, and he was washed off.

One of the hands, named Robert Pettengill, was taken by the same wave, and caught hold of the captain, both clinging together as they went down. When the vessel capsized the cook was immediately drowned. The mate tried to save him, but unsuccessfully.

The survivors clung to the wreck till 8 o'clock in the morning, when they were taken off. Mr. Daniel Mitchell, who lives on the Cape, took them in and cared for them, the mate and one of the hands, by the name of Duncan, having their limbs badly frozen.

The names of the crew were as follows:

> Captain J. C. PERRY.
> Mate E. T. ACHORN.
> Cook EUGENE DECROW.
> Crew FRED DUNCAN and ROBERT C. PENDLETON.

All belonged to Lincolnville. Capt. PERRY was about 42 years of age and leaves a wife and two children. The cook, MR. DECROW, was about 25 years of age, and leaves a wife and one child. MR. PENDLETON was unmarried.

New York Herald New York 1869-12-09

Cambridge

248 foot Passenger Steamer

On her regular passage from Boston to Bangor she ran aground on Old Man Ledge, 5 miles SSW of Port Clyde.

Steamer Cambridge

Anne C Maguire - 1886

Hit so hard it shook the lighthouse

There are times when it was not clear why a ship had wrecked. On the night of December 24, 1886, Weather Bureau journals show that at **Portland** there was a 20 mph wind and a light rain.

The Anne C. Maguire on the ledges at Portland Head lighthouse on Christmas Eve 1886. The vessel hit so hard she shook the lighthouse. The crew was saved but the ship was a total loss.

Though the crew of the Annie C. Maguire had seen the Portland Head Light through the rain, the schooner struck the rocks less than 100 feet from the lighthouse. The captain stated that he had lost his bearings and did not realize they were so near shore. Captain Thomas O'Neil, his family, and crew made it to safety with the help of the lighthouse keeper and his son.

SUSAN P. THURLOW - 1897

Six Sailors Drowned.

Total wreck of the schooner Susan P. Thurlow off Maine's coast. Only one man escaped death. He clung to a spar until finally thrown on the beach by the waves, the acting captain and the mate among those lost.

Portland, Me., Dec. 16. -- The schooner SUSAN P. THURLOW, bound from Hillsboro, N.B., for New York, with a cargo of plaster rock, went to pieces on Cushing Island, and the acting captain and five members of the crew were lost.

Ship Similar to the Susan P. Thurlow

One sailor managed to reach the land, and he informed the inhabitants of the wreck. The Thurlow was built in Harrington, Me., and hailed from New York.
The single survivor of the disaster is E. REIMANN.

He tells the story of the wreck as follows:
The Thurlow encountered rough weather off the Maine coast Tuesday night, and as the storm increased the captain decided to make Portland harbor, for shelter. He was only a few miles out from Portland when the rudder rope parted, and the vessel became disabled and was left at the mercy of a heavy sea. The

captain and crew tried to repair the steering gear, but even while they were thus engaged the schooner struck on the reef.

All three masts were carried away by the force of the impact, one of the topmasts striking the captain and crushing one of his legs. The captain and mate ordered the men to jump for their lives. REIMANN was caught by a huge wave and hurled into the sea. He was washed upon the beach on the island three times, but was unable to obtain a foothold and was swept back by the undertow. He managed to get hold of one of the spars and clung to it for a long time, finally being carried upon the beach by the waves.

He lay on the beach, benumbed with cold, and exhausted by his battle with the waves, for some time. At length he dragged himself in the hut of a fisherman, where he was cared for until morning, when he was brought to this city, and the story of the disaster became known.

The bodies of the acting captain, Mate McLEAN and three sailors were washed ashore on the island during the night. Nothing was left of the vessel in the morning. The beach is strewn with spars and other wreckage.

Daily Times New Brunswick New Jersey 1897-12-16

Edward J. Lawrence - 1925

320' 6-Masted Schooner

Built in Bath Maine - Burned and sank December 27, 1925 in **Portland** Harbor.

Bay State, Steamer - 1916

All's well that ends well

Built in 1895 at Bath, Maine and ran aground in a fog on September 23, 1916 at **Cape Elizabeth**, just off McKinley's Point. No fatalities.

In September 1916, the Portland Lightship went in for repairs. Usually it was replaced with a similar looking vessel, but this time a buoy was used instead.

On September 23, a thick fog contributed to Captain Foren mistaking the temporary buoy for the Old Anthony bell buoy that is located four miles further out to sea. This error caused

him to alter the ships course, and consequently the steamer Bay State ran aground on Holycomb Reef.

The ship could not be floated off the rocks, and though the water in the area was rough, all aboard were safely evacuated.

Cabin Cruiser DON - 1941

Recover Five Bodies From Missing Boat

Harpswell, Me., July 1 (AP) -- Recovery of five women's bodies, one of them burned, gave mute evidence today the the cabin cruiser Don with 35 aboard had gone down in lower Casco Bay after an explosion.

A motor vehicle operator's license found in the clothing of one of the women bore the name "ANN BERNICE STASULIS, 2 Holyoke avenue, Rumford, Me."

MISS STASULIS was known to be in the party which set out from Dyer's cove, Grea island, Sunday morning for Monhegan island, 40 miles to the eastward.

Twenty men and boys and 15 women were in the Don, commanded by Capt. PAUL JOHNSON, veteran East Harpswell fisherman. Most of the party lived in Rumford and adjacent Mexico.

The Don was reported to have reached Monhegan safely, indicating the cruiser was homeward bound, through fogbound waters, when its party met death.

MISS STASULIS' body was found in the water of Jacquish island, several miles seaward from Bailey island, in lower Casco bay. Men in WILL MUNSEY'S boat found MISS STASULIS' body and that of another young woman, about the same age -- in the early twenties.

None of the other five bodies were immediately identified. Two washed ashore at Dyer's cove; another was found in the water a mile and a half southwest of Bailey island; another off the east shore of than island.

MRS. ROBERT PLATTS, who found the body on the east shore, also found near it a red sweater. Exactly what happened to the boat was unknown. The sea had been calm since the craft left Sunday, but the coast had been enveloped in a thick, "dungeon" fog since Sunday night.

MISS STASULIS' wrist watch had stopped at 11:40 -- the

same time as that of a watch found on the wrist of the body found by JOHNSON.

OUELLETTE said he "thought" the watches probably stopped at 11:40 p. m. last night, but gave no explanation hor his belief.

The fog shut down over the coast about 11 p.m. Sunday. The bow section was found off **Ragged Island, Casco Bay**, ME

The Portsmouth Herald New Hampshire 1941-07-01

37 DROWNED OFF YACHT

Harpswell, Me., July 2 -- (AP) -- The 44-foot motorboat Don was pictured today by State Fisheries Warden JOHN STEVENS as a jinx ship that was "overcrowded" when it exploded and sent 37 men and women picnickers to death Sunday.

Declaring the Don had "sunk three times in the past decade" only to be raised, STEVENS told newsmen the craft was "topheavy" and that it carried 150 gallons of gasoline, some in cans on deck, when it set out of its last voyage to Monhegan Island, 20 miles away.

He added that is was inadequately equipped with life preservers for the party of Rumford and Mexico, Me., residents.

None of the first nine recovered bodies -- two men and seven women -- bore life preservers when they were picked up yesterday in the waters along the shores of Casco Bay. Two other bodies were held aboard fog-bound search craft overnight.

With every indication that there were no survivors of the trip that started so gaily, the disaster took the highest toll of life in New England waters since 47 perished in the Mackinac tragedy in Narragansett Bay, R. I., 16 years ago.

Indiana Evening Gazette Pennsylvania 1941-07-02

USS S-21 (SS-126) - 1945

219' Submarine first to measure Earth's gravity

USS S-21 was built at Quincy Shipyard in 1923 and used by the US Navy to obtain gravity measurements from around the world. Such measurements required the stability and lack of motion only attainable at sea on a submerged submarine.

USS S-21

Today such measurements are made through the use of satellites. The latest Earth Gravity Map is the most accurate model of gravity fluctuations around the world. It was recorded by the European Space Agency's GOCE satellite, whose instruments show Earth as a lumpy, multi-colored mesh of high and low points.

That's because gravity is not the same at all points on Earth; more massive features, such as the Rocky Mountains, have a stronger pull.

The ship was sunk on March 23, 1945 while being used as a Target Ship in Casco Bay. She now lies in one hundred and fifty feet of water off **Cape Elizabeth**

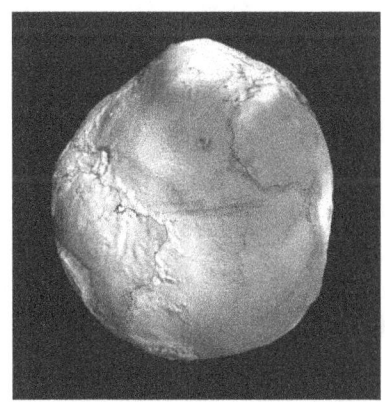

Earth Gravity Map from Satellite

Oakey L Alexander - 1947

368' Freighter broke in half

The ship was caught in a 80 mile per hour gale on March 3, 1947 and broke in half. The stern section is located just

Oakey L. Alexander hard aground, Cape Elizabeth, 1947

offshore of McKinney's Point, near High Head, **Cape Elizabeth** in about twenty feet of water. Rescuers on the shore, about two hundred yard away, shot a line to the ship that was then secured to the bridge. As breakers pounded against the stranded vessel, the crew crossed above the swirling whitewater on a system of lines and pulleys. Over a tense two hour period, all thirty-one men aboard were safely evacuated.

The Alexander, an American registered cargo ship of 5,284 gross reg tons, owned by the Pocahontas Steamship Co., and skippered by Captain Raymond Lewis, was having slow going in it's fight against the raging seas. The large ship was on top of a huge wave when a sudden lurch was felt throughout. Capt Lewis and the men on the bridge watched in horror as a 130 ft long section of the bow broke clear off and almost immediately sank from sight.

The Alexander had recently had a new bulkhead installed just aft of the place where the hull had torn in two. This bulkhead, fortunately, kept the rest of the ship from flooding. Capt Lewis, realizing his good luck for the moment, yet still cognizant of his peril called for "slow ahead" on the engine. He immediately steered his vessel towards the shore realizing that was the only real hope for saving his men and himself.

The Alexander eventually reached the rock and boulder strewn shore of Cape Elizabeth. The ship grounded some distance from dry land admist jagged rocks on all sides. The sea immediately began to pound the huge steel vessel to pieces on the rocks. People on shore realized the situation and the life-saving crew from Cape Elizabeth arrived on the scene shortly and proceeded to deploy their gear for the rescue.

A small cannon known as a "Lyle gun" fired a projectile with a small rope messenger line. This was fired seaward until it landed on the ship. The ships crew pulled in the light line until the heavy reacue line was aboard the ship and secured high on the superstructure. The life-savers tighted their end of the line on the shore. A device known as a "breeches buoy", a sling capable of carrying one man at a time, was run out to the ship and officers and crew were saved from a would-be watery grave.

This incident goes down in the pages of history as one of the few times that great seamanship on the part of captain and crew, and heroic, valiant efforts by those on shore, manage to cheat the sea of its victims at the last moment.

Compiled from news accounts and the Maine Historical Society.

This was the same gale that wrecked the *Novadoc*

S S Novadoc - 1947

261" Freighter lost during a gale

The ship disappeared in a major storm at sea. All hands (24) were lost. The U.S. Coast Guard conducted a massive search for the *Novadoc*, but no wreckage, bodies or debris were ever found.

Their last distress call: "Taking on water, 22 miles east of **Portland,** ME."

S S Novadoc in calm waters

Shipwrecks
~~~
Mid Coast and Penobscot Bay

Wrecks - Boothbay to Penobscot Bay

1624 (March) *Little James*, Pinnace – at **Damariscove**

1635 (August 15) *Angel Gabriel,* Gallion– off **Pemaquid**

The *Angel Gabriel* sailed from England for Massachusetts as part of a small convoy. A bronze plaque at Pemaquid Point commemorates the wreck. Most onboard were lost

1750 (October 22) *Jubile*, Sloop – **Seal Island**

1770 (November) *Industry* - Definite location unknown – thought to be near **Kennebunk Beach**

1777 (September 10) *Unidentified*, sunk in battle - **Wiscasset**

1778 *Adams*, Ship of War - **Penobscot River, Hampden**

1778 *Pallas*, Brig – Privateer – **Penobscot River, Bucksport**

1779 – *Forty One American Naval Vessels* sunk or burned by the British in the Battle for New Ireland - **Penobscot River, Verona and Searsport**

1782 (December 28) *HMS Albany*, British Navy 16 gun Sloop-of-War – grounded on Northern Triangles (ledge), **Penobscot Bay**

Britain defending New Ireland from the Penobscot Expedition

Albany was part of a small British fleet that defeated an American naval force during the Penobscot Expedition of 1779. By 1782, she was declared unfit for battle and demoted to a prison ship. After discharging prisoners in Boston, she headed toward Penobscot where she was wrecked on the Triangles. For many years the wreck reportedly was visible at low water. Since *Albany* was a prison ship when she wrecked, she probably no longer had guns on board.

1827 (November) *Garland*, Schooner - **Boothbay**

1814 (August) *Adams*, Frigate – **Penobscot River, Hampden**

1814 (September 14) *Unknown*, Frigate, **Penobscot River, Hampden** – Sunk in the Battle of Hampden 1 killed, 11 wounded, 70 prisoners captured

1836 (October 25) *Royal Tar* a/k/a "Circus Ship", Steamship - near **Vinalhaven**

1839 (December 21) *Charles,* Schooner - **Thomaston**

1839 (December 21) *Jordon l Mott,* Schooner - **Thomaston**

1851 (December 5) *Trojan, Schooner* – on **Cranberry Island**

1854 (December 10) *Eastern State,* Schooner – off **Pemaquid Point**

1855 (February) *Fame,* Schooner –near **Rockland**

1855 (February 23) *Visscher,* Schooner - **Boothbay**

1855 (April) *Ulysses,* Steamer- near **Rockland**

1855 (August 15) *Perseverance,* Schooner – **Seal Island**

City of Richmond sinks

1855 (December 9) *Uranus,* Schooner - **Searsport**

1856 (July 14) *Samuel,* Schooner – near **Castine**

1856 (December 20) *Conquest,* Schooner - off **Isle du Haut**

1857 (August) *Empress Baltimore,* Schooner – **Tenants Harbor**

1875 (January 14) *Georgia, Cargo Ship* - Northern Triangles ledge, **Penobscot Bay** near **Port Clyde**

1881 (April 30) *City of Richmond,* Steamer – near **North Haven**

1866 (March 28) *Marcena Johnson,* Cargo Ship – near **Castine**

1866 (May 22) *Uncle Sam*, Excursion Boat – near **New Harbor**

1886 (November 29) *Albert Jameson*, Schooner – near **Port Clyde**

1872 (May 28) *Emperor*, Steamer - **Seal Island**

1875 (January 14) *Georgia*, Steamer - **Northern Triangles** (ledge), **Penobscot Bay**

1878 (January 11) *Ulysses*, Sidewheel Steamer - Broke from moorings in gale at night, ran onto rocks and broke up – **Rockland Harbor**

1878 (January 11) *Island Belle*, Sloop – **Rockland Harbor**

1878 (August 31) *Lizzie & Namari*, Schooner – on **Manticus Island**

1881 (January 10) *Highflyer*, Schooner - near **Vinalhaven**

1779 (August 13) *Defense,* Privateer Brig - **Stockton Harbor**, near **Sears Island** She was scuttled to avoid being captured by the pursuing British Navy during the infamous Penobscot Expedition

1881 (August 30) *City of Richmond*, Coastal steamer (Side-wheeler) - south ledge of **Mark Island, Penobscot Bay**

Ship similar to *Defense*

1884 (May 8) *City of Portland*, Passenger Steamer - off **Owls Head**

1886 (February 10) *Cambridge*, Passenger Steamer - Boston and Bangor Line – on Old Man Ledge, 5 miles SSW of **Port Clyde**

1887 (January 4) *Lettie Wells*, Schooner - **Port Clyde**

1887 (January 15) *Afton*, Schooner - on **Cranberry Island**

1887 (August 15) *Nathan Clifford*, Schooner –in **Boothbay**

1888 (January) *Riverside,* Schooner – near **Stonington**

1888 (January 10) *Ulysses,* Steamer - near **Rockland**

1888 (July 4) *Mower,* Schooner - on **Manticus Island**

1888 (November 25) *Higgins,* Schooner – **North Haven**

1888 (November 25) *Mountain Fawn,* Schooner – **Naskeag Harbor**

1888 (November 25) *Golden Eagle,* Schooner – **Owl's Head**

1888 (November 25) *William McLoon,* Schooner – **Rockland Harbor**

1888 (November 25) *S. F. Mayer,* Schooner – **Rockland Harbor**

1888 (November 25) *Fannie May,* Lobster boat, – **Rockland Harbor**

Helen B Crosby **on ledge**

1888 (November 25) *Georgietta,* Schooner – **Spruce Head**

1888 (November 25) *Alida,* Schooner – **Ash Island Bar**

1888 (November 25) *Anna W. Barker,* Schooner – **Southern Island**

1888 (November 25) *Unknown,* Schooner – **Martinsville**

1888 (November 25) *Ella F, Crowell,* Schooner – **Vineyard Haven**

1888 (November 25) *James A. Brown,* Schooner – **Vineyard Haven**

1888 (November 25) *E. G. Willard,* Schooner – **Vineyard Haven**

1888 (November 25) *Bertha E. Glover,* Schooner – **Vineyard Haven**

1888 (November 25) *Idella Small,* Schooner – **Owl's Head**

1888 (November 25) *Robert Ripley,* Schooner – **Dolliver's Neck**

1888 (November 25) *Hurricane,* Steamer – **Vineyard Haven**

1888 (December 5) *Sinbad*, Schooner - near **Owls Head**

1889 (April) Agnes, Schooner - near **Owls Head**

1890 (December 19) *Carch*, Schooner – off **Deer Isle**

1890 (March 18) *S K F James*, Schooner – near **Stonington**

1890 (May 10) *Annie Sargent*, Schooner - **Boothbay**

1890 (August 27) *Fred Smith*, Schooner – **Port Clyde**

1890(October 24) *Mabel,* Schooner – off **Isle du Haut**

1890 (November 14) *Erie,* Schooner – near **Newcastle**

1891 (February 12) *James Rouke*, Schooner – off **Rockport**

1891 (March 15) *Augustus J Fabena*, Schooner - in **Boothbay**

1891 (September 30) *Clytie,* Schooner - on **Manticus Island**

Pemaquid Point Lighthouse

1891 (October 22) *Hattie M Crowell* – near **New Harbor**

1891 (October 29) *Empress, Schooner* – near **Boothbay Harbor**

1891 (November 29) *Albert Jameson*, Schooner – **Monhegan Island**

1895 (September 12) *Corinne*, Naval Vessel –near **Little Deer Isle**

1903 (September 17) *George F. Edmunds* – **Pemaquid Point**

1903 (September 17) *Sadie and Lillie, Two-masted coaster* – **Pemaquid Point**

1904 (September 14) *William H Archer*, Schooner – off **Islesboro**

1905 (May 30) *J Nickerson*, Schooner – off **Swans Island**

1905 (July 18) *Catalina*, Schooner - near **Rockland**

1905 (October 28) *Kentucky*, Schooner - **Sargentville**

1906 (January 17) *Atalanta*, Brig - **Seal Island**

1906 (September 9) *Metamora*, Schooner – near **New Harbor**

1906 (February 2) *Yankee Maid*, Schooner - **Seal Island**

1906 (April 28) *Wm F Campbell*, Schooner – off **Owls Head**

1906 (October 11) *Helen B Crosby*, Schooner – Grounded on ledge and later broke up - **Inner Bay Ledges**, 3 miles east of **Owls Head**

1907 (January 19) *Maude Malloch*, Schooner - near **Owls Head**

1907 (April 18) *Sardinian*, Schooner – off **Metinic Island**

1907 (November 16) *Ella Rose*, Schooner - near **Vinalhaven**

1907 (December 30) *Agnes V Gleason*, Schooner - in **Boothbay**

1908 (May 11) *Penobscott River*, Schooner – near **Stonington**

1908 May 23) *Cosmos*, Schooner – off **Isle du Haut**

1908 (August 7) *Three Sisters*, Cargo Ship – off **Isle du Haut**

1909 (July 1) *Alice E Clark*, Schooner – near **Isleboro**

1909 (October 10) James Boyce, Schooner - near **Owls Head**

1909 (October 13) *John Douglas*, Schooner – near **Owls Head**

Alice Clark on Islesboro Ledge

1910 (January 2) *Maud*, Schooner – off **Deer Isle**

1910 May 21) *S L Foster*, Schooner – off **Deer Isle**

1910 (June 29) *Henry L Peckham*, Schooner – near **Islesboro**

1910 (December 18) *Matiana*, Schooner - near **Rockland**

1911 (July 28) *Henry Chase*, Schooner - near **Port Clyde**

1911 (August 9) *Eleazer Boynton*, Schooner - near **Rockland**

1911 (September 3) *David Faust*, Schooner - near **Port Clyde**

1911 (October 10) *Emily A Staples*, Schooner - near **Port Clyde**

1912 *Corinna*, Steam ship built 1899, burned 1912 - **Brooksville**

1912 (January 5) *New Boxer*, Schooner – off **Isle du Haut**

1912 (January 10) Carolyn, Cargo Ship – nerar **Port Clyde**

1912 (September 29) *Catherine Enos*, Cargo Ship – off **Isle du Haut**

Joseph S Zeman

1912 (November 7) *William Rice*, Schooner - in **Boothbay**

1913 (March 22*) L Snow Jr*, Schooner – off **Camden**

1913 (April 21) *Helena,* Schooner - near **Port Clyde**

1913 (May 30) *Fred C Holden,* Schooner – near **Newcastle**

1913 (July 13) *Charles H Sprague*, Schooner – on **Monhegan Island**

1915 (May 27) *W G Butman*, Cargo Ship – off **Rockport**

1915 (August 7) *David Wallace*, Schooner - on **Manticus Island**

1914 (October 29) *Irvington*, Tug - **Northeast Pond Ledge** - 5 miles south of **Owl's Head**

1916 *Laura J*, Steamer - **Brooksville**

1916 (March 7) *Edward Stewart*, Schooner - on **Cranberry Island**

1916 (October 21) *Eliza Levensaler*, Schooner - on **Monhegan Island**

1917 (March 17) *Cumberland*, Schooner – near **Vinalhaven**

1918 (September 13) *Lottie O Merchant* – near **Newfound Ground**

1918 (October) *Mary Weaver*, Schooner - **Boothbay**

1919 (May 23) *Wm O Hilton*, Schooner - near **Rockland**

1920 (February 6) *Polias*, Cargo Ship - Struck **Old Cilley Ledge** in blizzard, eleven casualties - near **Port Clyde**

1921 (June 8) *Rozella*, Tanker - near **Port Clyde**

1921 (October 5) *Seth Nyman*, Schooner – off **Isle du Haut**

1921 (November) *McCormick*, Tanker –**Kennebec River**

1922 (February 3) *Joseph S Zeman*, 5 Masted Schooner - off **Metinic Island**

1923 (September 20) *Richard,* Sloop – near **Bath**

1924 (November 17) *Canisteo*, Schooner - Barge - **Monhegan Island**

1924 (November 17) *Pohatcong,* Schooner - Barge - **Monhegan Island**

Polias

1924 (November 17) *Strafford,* Schooner - **Monhegan Island**

1924 (November 23) *S T Co No 5*, Barge – near **Belfast**

1925 *F C Pendleton*, Schooner – near **Islesboro**

1925 (October 10) *Richardson,* Schooner Barge - near **Rockland**

1926 (November 27) *Emily F Northam*, Schooner - on **Cranberry Island**

1927 *Edna M McKnight*, Schooner - in **Boothbay**

1927 (November 4) *Georgia O Jenkins*, Fishing Boat - **Vinalhaven**

1928 (September 15) *Olive Etta*, Schooner - in **Boothbay**

1929 (January 14) Wawenock, Schooner – near Isle au Haut

1930 (July 4) *Gardner G Deering*, Schooner 5- masted built 1903, burned 1930 – **Brooksville**

1931 (September 12) *Meddo No 1*, Freighter – **Bucksport**

1931 (September 12) *Meddo No 2*, Freighter – **Bucksport**

1932 Hesper - **Wiscasset**

1932 (August 3) *L V Ostrom*, Cargo Ship – near **Camden**

1933 (April 2) *Charlotte L Morgan*, Schooner - near **Tenants Harbor**

1933 (April 2) *Cameo*, Schooner - **Bucksport**

1934 *Eva and Belle*, Steamer - **Brooksville**

1935 (June 8) *Castine*, Excursion boat – Inner Bay Ledges, **Vinalhaven Island**

1836 (October 25) *Royal Tar*, Coastal Side-wheeler –Vessel caught fire east of **Vinalhaven Island**

1938 (March 28) *Cullen No 18*, Brig - **Searsport**

1938 (November 10) Vinalhaven, Steamer - near **Rockland**

Castine

1939 *Cora F Cressy*, Schooner – near **Tenants Harbor**

1940 (January 24) *Emma* – near **Vinalhaven**

1942 (January1) *Diablesse*, Cargo Ship – near **Brookville**

1942 (March 15) *William L Putman*, Steamer - **Seal Island**

1943 (August 8) *St Rosalie*, Steamer - **Monhegan Island**

1943 (May 5) *Hartwelson*, Freighter - Sunk near Bantam Rock, 8 miles south of **Boothbay Harbor**

1945 (September 14) *Grace and Rosalie,* Schooner - on **Cranberry Island**

Cargo Ship Sinking

1948 (November 5) *D. T. Sheridan,* Tug – **Monhegan Island**

1952 (December 16) *Evzone,* Tanker - on **Manticus Island**

1953 (May 9) *St Bernadette,* Cargo Ship – off **Swans Island**

1963 (December 18) *G L 142,* Barge - near **Rockland**

1977 (December 24) *Badir,* Cargo Ship – **Bucksport**

1899 (October) *Bay State SS,* British Cargo Ship – off **Cape Elizabeth**

Sailing Ship Going Down

Stories and Tales

Mid Coast and Penobscot Bay

Little James - 1624

Plymouth Colony's Pinnace

The wreck of the *Little John* is one of the earliest recorded wrecks. *Little James* arrived at the Plymouth Colony from England in 1623. Many of the passengers were the wives and children of the Mayflower settlers that had been left behind when the *Mayflower* departed in 1620.

She was wrecked at Damariscove in March of 1624 while on a fishing trip. This area was well known to the Pilgrims because when the Pilgrims of Plymouth Colony were facing starvation in the spring of 1622, they sent a boat to Damariscove to beg for assistance. The fishermen there responded by filling the colonists boat with cod which helped ensure the Pilgrim's survival.

The then governor of the Plymouth Colony, William Bradford wrote of this event in his book "Of Plymouth Plantation, 1620-1647". . . *"They having some trouble and charge new-masted and rigged their pinnace, in the beginning of March they sent her well victualed to the eastward on fishing.*

Ship similar to *Little James*

She arrived safely at a place near Damariscove, and was there well harbored, in a palce where ships used to ride, there being some ships already arrived out of England. But shortly there arose such a violent and extraordinary storm, as the seas broke over such places in the harbor as was never seen before, and drove her against great rocks, which beat such a hole in her bilge as a horse and cart might have gone in, and after drove her into deep water, where she lay sank.

The master was drowned, the rest of the men, all save one, saved their lives with much ado; all her provisions, salt, and whatever else was in her was lost.

Angel Gabriel – 1635

240 Ton Passenger Galleon

Angel Gabriel was one in a fleet of five ships, the *James*, the *Elizabeth* (*Bess*), the *Mary* and the *Diligence*. Approaching New England, they were hit by the "Great Colonial Hurricane of 1635". The *James* and the *Angel Gabriel* tried to ride out the storm just off the coast of modern-day Hampton, New Hampshire.

According to the ship's log and the journal of Increase Mather, whose father Richard Mather and family were on the *James*, the following was recorded;

Gallion similar to *Angel Gabriel*

At this moment,... their lives were given up for lost; but then, in an instant of time, God turned the wind about, which carried them from the rocks of death before their eyes. ...her (James) sails rent in sunder, and split in pieces, as if they had been rotten ragges...

They tried to stand down during the storm just outside the Isles of Shoals, but the *James* lost all three anchors, as no canvas or rope would hold, but on Aug 13, 1635, torn to pieces, and not one death, all one hundred-plus passengers aboard the *James* managed to make it to Boston Harbor two days later.

The *Angel Gabriel* was wrecked off the coast of Maine, but the smaller, faster ships, the *Mary*, the *Bess*, and the *Diligence* outran the storm, and landed in Newfoundland on August 15, 1635 and the *James* made it to Boston Harbor on the same day.

A plaque commemorating the loss was dedicated August 8, 1965 at Pemaquid Point, Maine.

Industry – 1700

Lost on Maiden Voyage

She was built at Packard's Rock, now known as Cushing, Maine. She was launched late in November and set sail for Boston. That was the last anyone ever heard of her or any of the persons on board.

No one knows what happened to the ship. There were not storms or foul weather to threaten her. However, a short time after her launch wreckage began coming ashore from Cape Porpoise, Maine to Cape Ann in Massachusetts.

Some believe her remains began to appear out of the sand at Kennebunk Beach in 1960 but were quickly re-covered with sand by a Nor' easter.

Albany – circa 1778

British Sloop of War

The *Albany* was wrecked somewhere between Mussel Ridges and Green Island in Penobscot Bay in an area known as the Northern Triangles.

Legend has it that the crew abandoned ship and began rowing towards Castine but became disoriented in the fog and eventually landed at Matinicus Island but not before three of the men had frozen to death.

British Sloop of War

The surviving crewmen, frost bitten and half dead, were taken into the homes of the islanders that these same sailors had raided the island three months earlier.

Adams – 1814

United States Frigate

While freeing the ship from a ledge near the Isle au Haut and after floating off the rocks they proceeded up the Penobscot River to the town of Hampden. While there the captain learned of the capture of Castine by the British.

In order to prevent the Adams from falling into the hands of the British, Captain Morris ordered the ship be blown up thereby preventing it from falling into enemy hands.

Captain Morris had a very distinguished career. He was the commanding officer aboard the USS Constitution and, as Navy Commissioner, supervised the Naval Academy at Annapolis for many years.

The Castine – 1935

Went aground on Seal Ledge

The captain had stopped his engines because of the thick fog when suddenly the ship began to list at an alarming angle. Scores of passengers slid into the icy cold waters of the Bay; four drowned.

Lobster boats and many other craft came in response to the ship's distress signal and many lives were saved. The ship broke in two shortly after the last passenger was saved.

In true Yankee fashion, "Waste not, want not", the bow section was salvaged and used to construct a unique cottage on the shore at Treasure Island, Vinalhaven.

The Castine

Royal Tar – *1836*

a/k/a *Circus Ship-*
Coastal Steamer Side-wheeler

In October 1836 *Royal Tar* was booked to take a traveling circus-including an elephant named Mogul, a Bengal tiger, a zebra, a hyena, two lions, two dromedaries and assorted smaller animals-from Yarmouth, Nova Scotia to Portland, Maine. There were also 90 passengers and crew. Two of the ship's four lifeboats were removed to make room for the animals.

Royal Tar ablaze at sea
Peabody Essex Museum painting

Fire broke out and began to consume the ship, the captain attempted to beach his vessel on the eastern shore of **Vinalhaven**. He never made it.

Some passengers managed to get off *Royal Tar* in the remaining two lifeboats, though 31 drowned.

The U.S. Revenue Cutter Service vessel *Veto* arrived and rescued 60 people. Most of the animals swam frantically around the boat, eventually drowning. Others perished in their cages. The body of Mogul, the elephant, was found floating near **Brimstone Island** a few days later.

Georgia - 1875

Civil War blockade runner

Built as the *Japan*, she was purchased secretly by the Confederate States government in 1863. She left the yard as a merchant ship, was armed at sea (off France) and renamed the *CSS Georgia*.

The vessel served as a blockade runner and raider during the Civil War until captured by the Union *USS Niagra* off Portugal.

Georgia as a Confederate Blockade Runner

After the war she was converted to a merchant ship, renamed *SS Georgia* and sold to a Canadian company. She was wrecked while on a routine trip from Halifax to Portland in 1875.

Steamer *City of Portland* – 1884
Wrecked Off Owl's Head

The Steamship City of Portland wrecked on a shoal off Rockland, Maine, during the early morning hours of May 8, 1884. An estimated 70 passengers miraculously escaped injury and death in the incident.

The 1,000-ton vessel ran aground at Northwest Ledge, **Owl's Head**, at 3:15 a.m.

Portland at Sea

A New York newspaper claimed the steamer had 70 passengers onboard plus cargo when it left Portland at 8:45 p.m. the previous day.

As the morning hours progressed, the weather became threatening so the second in command altered course without informing the Captain, choosing to steer through Grindstone Channel and pass between Sheep and Fisherman's Islands.

The buoy marking the way was not in its proper place and while running at a full speed the City of Portland crashed its wooden hull right on top of Grindstone Ledge before coming to an abrupt stop.

The ship was an obvious wreck. Because it was hard on the rocks, it did not slide back into deep water to sink, thus giving the crew and passengers time to escape.

Cumberland, Tug

87' Tug

She was built in 1910 at Rockland, ME and owned by Snow Marine Company.

While leaving Vinalhaven Harbor (Carvers Harbor) in a gale, with a heavily-laden barge in tow, the tow cable snagged in the tug's propeller and the vessel was driven by heavy seas onto the point of Green Island.

Cumberland under way

The *Cumberland* was exposed to the full fury of the gale and quickly went to pieces on the rocks. The barge was badly damaged but apparently survived the incident.

Amarato - 1985

Scuttled by Thieves off Owls Head in 1985

The 71' Amaretto (formerly the Muriel). NF correspondent Joe Upton used to own the 68-year-old sardine carrier and wrote about her this year in our January-June issues.
— Boutilier photo

Amaretto

A H WHITMORE -1903

ASHORE IN COLLISION

Schooner A. H. Whitmore Has Full Share of Hard Luck.

Rockland, Me., May 1--The schooner A. H. Whitmore, from Stonington to Portland with granite, ran aground, today, in the Fox Island thoroughfare and a half hour later was badly damaged in collision with the schooner Abbie Schlafer, Capt. Peterson, bound from Stonington to New York with stone.

The Schlafer passed within two feet of the stranded schooner and carried away the stern gear, main boom and mainsail of the Whitmore, proceeding with the gear on her bow without investigating the extent of the damage. The Whitmore was towed here. Capt. B. F. Pascal of Stonington, owner of the Whitmore, had demanded damaged form Farrand & Spear of Rockland, owners of the Schlaefer.

Daily Kennebec Journal, Augusta, ME 2 May 1903

J M KENNEDY - 1903

THE CREW ESCAPED

Schooner J. M. Kennedy a Total Wreck on "Old Man's" Ledge.

Rockland, Me., May 1--The two-masted schooner J. M. Kennedy, Capt. Hutchins of Ellsworth, bound from Rondout, N. Y., with 1400 barrels of cement for Cooper & Co., Belfast, was wrecked during the gale early Friday on the "Old Man" ledge off Port Clyde and is a total loss. Capt. Hutchins and crew of three men escaped in their life boat to Port Clyde and were brought here. The Kennedy was owned by Joseph Higgins of Ellsworth, was of 120 tons, 87 feet long and 15 feet beam and seven feet deep. She was built at Ellsworth in 1869.

Daily Kennebec Journal, Augusta, ME 2 May 1903

D. T. Sheridan, Tug - 1924

The Sheridan was towing barges when she grounded on rocks in dense fog and beached on rocks in **Lobster Point, Monhegan Island** on November 5th

She was a total loss and her remains are still visible at low tide at Lobster Point, Monhegan Island,

D T Sheridan aground

Admiral Peary's SS Roosevelt

Built on Verona Island - 1904

Admiral Peary designed his ship, the *S.S. Roosevelt*, to withstand the extreme conditions of the Arctic. Construction of the Roosevelt began on October 15, 1904 and she was launched on March 23, 1905 from Verona Island, Maine. The *Roosevelt* carried Peary and his crew on the successful 1909 voyage to the North Pole.

After 1909, a series of owners used the Roosevelt for a variety of purposes. She served as a salvage vessel, a fishing boat, and a tug boat. During World War I the S.S. Roosevelt was used to patrol the West Coast.

Admiral Peary's SS Roosevelt

Battle for *New Ireland:*

The Penobscot Expedition

July 25 to August 15, 1779

The Penobscot Expedition - 1779

The **Penobscot Expedition** was an American naval expedition sent to reclaim Maine, which the British had conquered and renamed *New Ireland*. It was the largest American naval expedition of the American Revolutionary War and is sometimes thought the United States' worst naval defeat until Pearl Harbor. The fighting took place both on land and on sea over a twenty two day period, in what is today Castine, Maine.

The military expedition consisted of a fleet of 19 armed vessels and 24 transports, carrying 344 guns, under Commodore Dudley Saltonstall, and a land force of about 1,200 men, under Gen. Solomon Lovell, seconded by Gen. Peleg Wadsworth. Lt. Col. Paul Revere in charge of the ordnance.

New ~~England~~ Ireland

In June 1779, British Army forces established a series of fortifications centered on a fort located on the Majabigwaduce Peninsula in Penobscot Bay, with the goals of establishing a military presence on that part of the coast and beginning a new colony to be known as *New Ireland*. In response, the state of Massachusetts, with some support from the Continental Congress, raised an expedition, known as the *Penobscot Expedition*, to drive the British out.

Fort George, Castine
British fort built to protect *New Ireland*

The Colonial Americans landed troops July 25, 1779 and attempted to establish a siege of the British fort in a series of actions seriously hampered by disagreements over control of the expedition between Commodore Dudley Saltonstall and General Solomon Lovell. The operation ended in disaster when a British fleet under the command of Sir George Collier arrived on August 13th, driving the American fleet to total self-destruction up the Penobscot River. The survivors of the American expedition were forced to make an overland journey back to more Massachusetts with minimal food and armament.

After the peace was signed in 1783, the New Ireland proposal was abandoned.

The Encounter

The little known Penobscot Expedition event in Revolutionary War history, took place from July 25 to August 15, 1779.

Painting depicting Britain defending New Ireland from the Penobscot Expedition during the American Revolution by Dominic Serres

That year the British were attracted to the Penobscot peninsula (Castine) for several reasons: as a possible Loyalist haven, as a source of timber for the King's Navy, and as a strategic naval base and coastal trading post. Early in June the English sent a small flotilla from Halifax, Nova Scotia, with approximately 750 troops to occupy the area and to build a fort, later named Fort George. Capt. Henry Mowat was in command of the naval vessels and Brig. Gen. Frances McLean the land forces. They arrived at the peninsula in mid-June.

Since Maine was a province of Massachusetts at that time, the occupation of Penobscot, and its potential as a British naval base, was of great concern to the Massachusetts General Assembly in Boston. In record time, an American fleet of 19 armed vessels and 24 transports, with more than 1,000 militia, was assembled and sent to Penobscot Bay to retake the area. Commodore Dudley Saltonstall was commander of the naval forces, Brig. Gen. Solomon Lovell had command of the land forces, with **Lt. Col. Paul Revere** in command of the ordnance train. The fleet reached the head of Penobscot Bay on July 25.

For two weeks there were a few brief, intense forays between the land forces but nothing decisive. Saltonstall, with his superior naval strength, was reluctant to take any action against Mowat's three-ship defense, which gave the British sufficient time to send for and receive reinforcements from New York.

Big Mistake

On August 13 seven heavily armed British warships, under the command of Sir George Collier, sailed into Penobscot Bay where they faced Saltonstall's fleet. Anticipating a sea battle, Lovell abandoned all his positions and began a retreat up the Penobscot River.

Frigate Ablaze in River

On the morning of August 14, to the astonishment of the American Lovell and Englishman Collier, Saltonstall, who had the guns of his ships bearing broadside on the advancing British, turned his ships about and fled up the river where his entire fleet of warships and transports were sunk or scuttled and burned by their own forces. The panic-stricken crews and troops, with most of their leaders, rushed to shore and into the forest where they made their way back to Boston.

Cost of Eight Million in Colonial Dollars

It was a frightful defeat. American forces had suffered 500 casualties. The failed Penobscot Expedition is estimated to have cost the revolutionaries eight million dollars, proved to be the greatest American naval defeat until Pearl Harbor in 1941. The loss in guns and supplies would never be accurately known.

Battle for New Ireland

The Stage is Set

June 16, 1779 – British invade Castine to establish New Ireland

A British force of three warships and six hundred fifty men arrive at Castine to erect a fort, to be named Fort George, for the purpose of controlling Eastern Maine and the Penobscot region.

June 19, 1779 - Colonialists respond

Boston receives word of the British invasion of Castine, then part of Massachusetts. An untrained and untested battle group is hastily assembled and departs heading to Castine to discharge the British from Colonial territory.

The force consists of 18 Warships, 19 troop transports and 3,300 men and the largest

Colonialist Fleet sets sail for Maine

force ever assembled by the colonialist. The fleet is under the command of Commodore Dudley Saltonstall. Generals Solomon Lovell and Peleg Wadsworth commanded the land forces with Lt Colonel Paul Revere in charge of the artillery.

July 24, 1779 – British learn the Colonial expedition is coming

British learn of the Americans imminent arrival and hastily attempt to finish and arm their still uncompleted fort, Fort Penobscot, and maneuver their 3 ship to best defend Castine Harbor.

The Penobscot Expedition's Order of Battle

July 25, 1779 – Americans Battle Group arrives in Penobscot Bay

Commodore Saltonstall attacks the British in Castine Harbor but is driven back.

July 28, 1779 – Americans land on Dice Head

American forces land at Dice Head capturing the British artillery battery there. They then fortified their position by building two fortifications.

Meanwhile, the British are doing the same on the peninsula.

No Overall Commander - In the haste to charter the commanders of the expedition, the Massachusetts legislators failed to appoint a Supreme Commander of the overall expedition.

Colonists attack British battery on Dice Head

Reluctant Commodore - The result; although the generals Lovell and Wadsworth might agree on a course of battle, they could not obtain artillery support from Commodore Saltonstall. It is reported that Saltonstall did not want to engage the British ships even thou he outnumbered then 18 to 1.

Rented Fleet – Others speculate that part of Saltonstall's hesitancy stemmed from the fact that much of his fleet was chartered or rented from wealthy and influential merchants and politicians and he feared the wrath the loss of their vessels might bring.

The result: the American commanders would argue and fight over the course of action they should take for the next seventeen days.

August 13, 1779 –British reinforcements arrive

A squadron, under the command of Sir George Collier, arrives in Penobscot Bay to support their comrades in Castine.

5 British War ships arrive

August 14, 1779 – Commodore Saltonstall attempts an attack

An effort to engage the British squadron was made and the Americans lay advantaged and able to "broadside" the advancing squadron. Much to the surprise and horror of generals and Lt Colonel Paul Revere, Saltonstall ordered a retreat up the Penobscot River rather than engage the British.

It is reported that shortly after the command was given to go up the river, the wind shifted disadvantaging the American fleet. As the British steadily approached the colonialists began running their ships aground, burning and scuttling them, then fleeing into the forest to begin a long 250 mile trek back to Boston without food or provisions.

The British capture 2 American warships and 9 transports while losing none of theirs. The British took 70 casualties and the Americans suffered 474 either killed, capture or missing in action.

August 15, 1779 – Maine residents flee

Searsport, Belfast, and other families in the area, flee in fear of being captured or killed by the British. The towns would not again be populated until after the war's end and a peace treaty is signed.

The Aftermath

The Colonial treasury of Massachusetts was drained and the commonwealth was broke. Commodore Saltonstall, generals Solomon Lovell and Peleg Wadsworth as well as Lt. Col. Paul Revere were later court-martialed, charged with cowardice and insubordination; the boards found Saltonsall guilty, but acquitted Revere and the others.

The Battle for New Ireland or The Penobscot Expedition would remain the largest loss of American Naval Vessels in a single engagement until the Japanese bombing attack on Pearl Harbor to begin WWII.

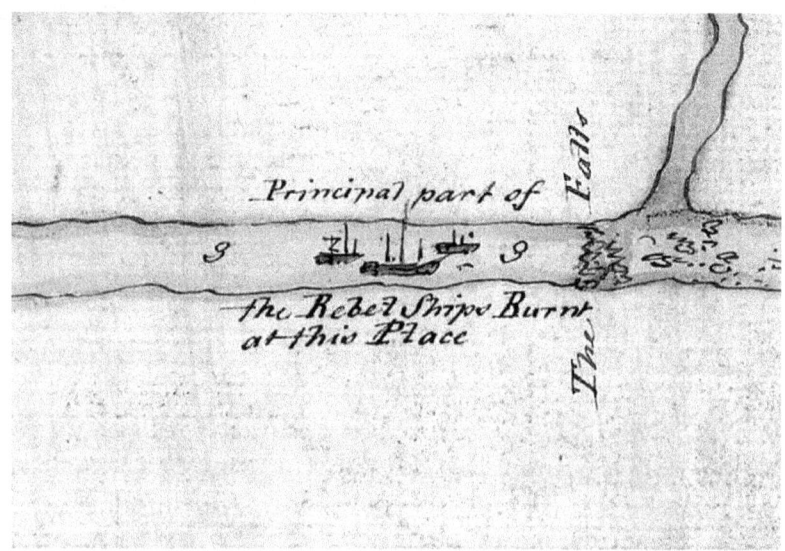

British map showing approximate location of burned Colonial ships below the Bangor waterfall

War of 1812 and the Battle of Hampden

Another Attempt by the British to Establish *New Ireland*

The **Battle of Hampden** involved the British conquering present-day Maine and establishing the colony *New Ireland* during the War of 1812. Sir John Sherbrooke led a British force from Halifax, Nova Scotia to re-establish *New Ireland*.

Sir John Sherbrooke

The Battle of Hampden occurred in August of 1814, concurrent with the retaking of Castine. A particularly brutal British Captain Robert Barrie, saw to it that after defeating a small local militia and sinking an American Frigate, Mainers would pay for their "crimes". His troops sacked the towns of Bangor and Hampden, burning, smashing and looting. When local leaders begged him to show a little humanity he said,

"Humanity! I have none for you. My business is to burn, sink, and destroy. Your town is taken by storm. By the rules of war we ought to lay your village in ashes, and put its inhabitants to the sword. But I will spare your lives, though I mean to burn your houses."

The Aroostook War of 1842

Maine/Canada border dispute

The Aroostook War, although devoid of actual military combat, involved heated arguments and negotiations. Neither America nor Britain actually wanted war as it would have greatly interfered with the two nations' trade.

Daniel Webster negotiated a compromise that was the basis of the *Webster-Ashburton Treaty* in 1842. This treaty settled the Maine-Canada boundary and the boundary between Canada and New Hampshire, Michigan and Minnesota.

Fort Knox, built 1844-1869

Built to defend against further British attacks

Tensions were high between the British and the Americans given the two attempts by the British to claim what is now "Downeast" Maine even though yet another Peace Treaty had just been negotiated.

The Fort's History

Fort Knox

The fort is located on the western bank of the Penobscot River in the town of Prospect, Maine, about 5 miles from the mouth of the river. It was the first fort in Maine built of granite (instead of wood). The purpose of the fort was to defend against further attacks from the British or others. Construction funding from Congress was intermittent, and although nearly a million dollars were spent, the fort's design was never fully completed. It is named after Henry Knox, the first US Secretary of War.

Ships Lost in the Battle for *New Ireland*

Colonial Vessels Lost in the Battle for *New Ireland*

August 14 1779

Some of the 43 Colonial American ships and transports lost in the Penobscot Expedition have been found. The Penobscot River between Bangor and Brewer has at least nine sites with ships involved in the Penobscot Expedition.

The Maine Historic Preservation Commission declares; "We've narrowed it down to 27 [sites] in the Penobscot River". Not all of the ships identity has been established.

> The New Hampshire privateer *Hampden* and the ship *Hunter*, one of the largest and best of the Massachusetts privateers, were captured by the British.
>
> *Active*, Brigantine – Privateer 30 Guns, 16 six pounders, 14 four pounders – near **Kenduskeag Stream, Bangor**
>
> *Black Prince* – Ship, Massachusetts Privateer – *Guns, 20-6 pounders* - near **Bangor/Brewer**
>
> *Defence*, Brig – Privateer – **Devereaux Cove in Stockton Springs**
>
> *Charming Sally*, Ship Massachusetts Privateer Guns, 20 9-pounders - near **Bangor/Brewer**
>
> *Diligent* Brig – Guns, 14 – 4 pounders – near **Bangor/Brewer**
>
> The *Diligent* was formerly the British warship HMB *Diligent*. She was captured off Sandy Hook, NJ in May of 1779 by the Continental Sloop *Providence*.
>
> *Hazard*, Brig – Massachusetts State Navy. Guns, 18 6 – Pounders - near **Bangor/Brewer**
>
> *Hector*, Ship – Massachusetts Privateer, Guns – 20-9 pounders - near **Bangor/Brewer**

Monmouth, Ship – Massachusetts Privateer, Guns, 20–6 pounders – near Bangor/Brewer

Pidgeon. Sloop – unarmed Transport - near **Bangor/Brewer**

Providence –Sloop of War – *Guns, 14-6 pounders* –She was the first vessel authorized for use by the Continental Navy (1775) and fired the first shot of the American Revolution. Providence was the first command of Col. John Paul Jones of "The British are coming" fame. near **Bangor/Brewer**

Putnam, Brig – Privateer - **Penobscot River**

Revenge, Sloop or Brig - **Penobscot River**

Sally, unknown – Privateer - **Penobscot River**

Samuel. - **Winterport**

Spring Bird, Paul Revere's Ship - **Frankfort**

Sky Rocket, Brig – Privateer, burned off **Verona**

A transport - mouth of the **Sedgeunkedunk Stream in South Brewer**

Tiranicide, Brig – Massachusetts State Navy – Guns, 20-6 pounders, near **Bangor/Brewer**

Vengence, Brig – Privateer - **Penobscot River**

Warren – **Winterport**

British Side of the Story

A British account of the battle has another 20 small vessels destroyed at the mouth of the Penobscot River near **Verona**, and **Searsport**.

*At 6 upewards of 20 **sail of small Vessels run on shore**, the most of them they set fire to, which Oblig'd us to anchor." At seven o'clock the **Greyhound** got into shoal water and anchored. About the same time the Americans set fire to a sloop and sent her down the river. "Sent 2 Boats man & armed, Cut her Loose & twod Her on shore; sent 3 Boats to Board a schooner & bring her to Anchor, she proved to be Laden with provisions.*

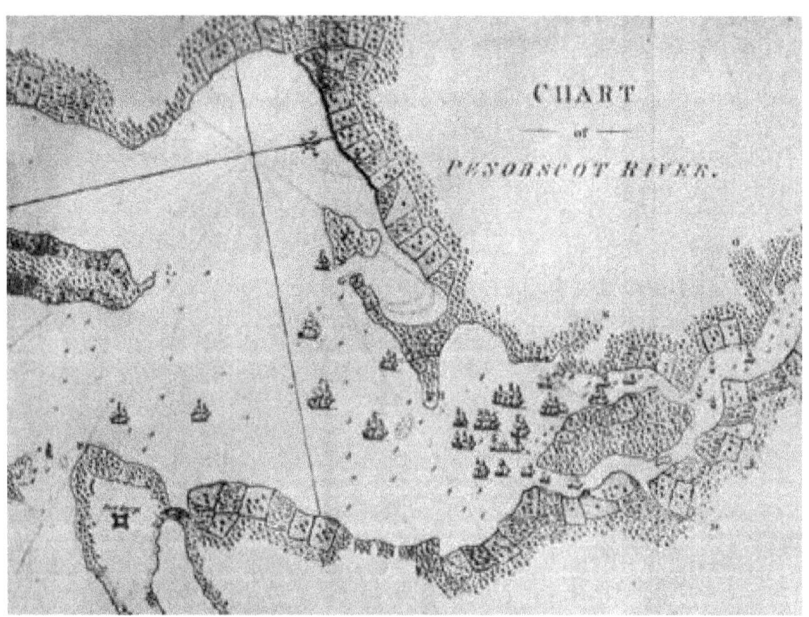

Colonial Naval forces bottled up off Verona Island

Remains of a 1779 ship?

Does this Google Earth satellite view reveal the outline of an ancient 1779 ship buried in Penobscot River's mud?

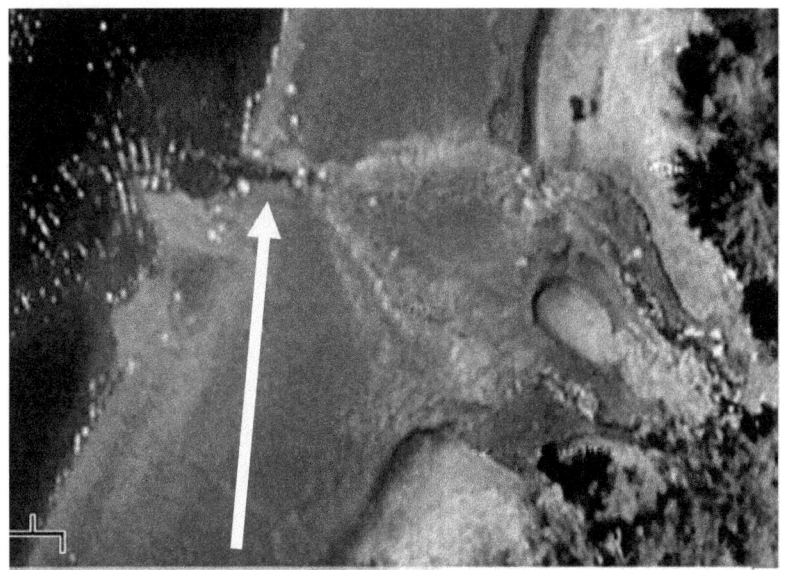

Outline of a Wreck in the Penobscot River

An on the ground view of the ship's skeleton sticking out of the mud.

Ship Parts Stick out of River's Mud

Photo by Deborah Copp Bouchard

Shipwrecks on Maine's *Bold Coast*

Mount Desert - Downeast

Shipwrecks Mount Desert – Downeast

1740 *Grand Design*, Passenger ship carrying Irish immigrants to America - **Mount Desert**

1755 (February 15) *H M S Halifax*, Schooner – **Foster Island**

Similar to Grand Design

1777 (August 13) *Unidentified* Privateer – **Bucks Harbor**

1826 (August 23) *New York*, Brig – off **Petit Manan Light**

1835 *Sarah* – off **Jonesport**

1846 (November) *North America*, Steamer – **Isle au Haut**

1851 (December) *Paragon*, Brig - **Schoodic Point**

1854 (September 21) *Brazil*, Brig – **West Quoddy Head**

1855 (March 1) *Roswell*, Brig - **West Quoddy Head**

1855 (April) *Elvira*, Schooner – near **Cutler**

1855 (April 11) *Marcellus*, Schooner - **West Quoddy Head**

1855 (June) *Melville*, Schooner - **Mount Desert**

1855 (June 19) *Ann Denman*, Schooner – off **Head Harbor Island**

1855 (September 17) *Abigail Gould*, Schooner - **Bar Harbor**

1855 (December 9) *Gov Arnold*, Schooner - **Machias**

1856 August 1) *Lubec*, Schooner - **Pembroke**

1856 (August 8) *Florence*, Schooner - **Machias**

1856 (August 9) *Claremont*, Schooner - **Machias**

1856 (December 17) *Flushing*, Paddle Steamer - **Machias**

1858 (July 11) *Wreath* – **Bass Harbor, Mount Desert**

1860 (March 24) *Ava*, Schooner – **Mount Desert**

1867 (October 23) *Pilot*, Schooner - **Mt. Desert**

1868 (June 22) *C.E. Howard*, Schooner - **Cranberry Isles**

1868 (October 25) Amaranth, Schooner - **Long Ledge**

1869, *Aerolite*, Bark - **Baker Island Bar** during a snowstorm

1872 (July 21) *Queen*, Paddle Steamer - **Eastport**

1876 Ernest, Schooner (a US government survey ship) – **Isle au Haut**

1876 (March 17) *Olive Clark*, Schooner – **Cranberry Isles**

1876 (26 Apr) *Redondo*, Schooner – **Bakers Island**

U. S. Coast and Geodetic Survey Schooner

1876 (28 June) *Sunbeam*, Schooner - **Calais**

1878 (4 November) *Presto*, Schooner - **Machias**

1878 (July 12) *Lilian Gertrude*, Schooner – **Seal Harbor**

1886 (November 30) *Water Lily*, Schooner – **Baker Island**

1887 *Highland Queen*, Schooner – **Scoodic Point**

1887 (January) *Afton*, Schooner **Baker Island Bar**

1887 (May 25) *R G Moran*, Schooner – **Seal Harbor**

1887 (September 17) *A G Blair*, Schooner – **Seal Harbor**

1888 (March 31) *Sedona*, Schooner – near **Libby Island**

1888 November 6) *J J Worthington*, Schooner – off **Mount Desert**

1889 (January 6) *Lillian B Jones*, Schooner – near **Corea**

1889 (July 1) *George Killam*, Schooner - **West Quoddy Head**

1889 (July 20) *Eduardo*, Freighter – off **Cutler**

1889 (October 9) *Delia Hinds*, Schooner – near **Bass Harbor**

1890 *Mabel*, Schooner – **Isle au Haut**

1890 (January 24) *Laurissa*, Schooner – near **Libby Island**

1890 January 25) *Ximena*, Schooner – near **Libby Island**

1890 (August 8) *Castillian* - **Bald Porcupine Island**

1890 (December 29) *G Stanley*, Schooner – **Quoddy Head**

1891 (June 1) *William Mason*, Schooner – **Machias Bay**

1891 (June 2) *Joseph W Fish*, Schooner – near **Eastport**

Quoddy Head Light
Most Eastern Point in the US

1891 (June 4) *Seabird*, Schooner - near **Libby Island**

1891 (July 6) *Pavillo*, Schooner - **West Quoddy Head**

1891 (December 18) *Mabel Purdy*, Schooner - **Machiasport**

1891 (December 28) *Huntress*, Schooner – near **Great West Island**

1892 (April 5) *Byrtle*, Schooner – **Baker Island**

1892 (November 10) *Burpee C*, Schooner – **Bar Harbor**

1900 *Nellie J Crocker* - **Schoodic Island**

1903 *Yreka*, Schooner – **Southwest Gap**

1902 (November 15) *Sadie*, Schooner- off **Cutler**

1904 (September) *Ida M*, Schooner – **Long Ledge**

1905 (May 13) *J Nickerson*, Schooner – off **Swans Island**

1905 (August 12) *Joe,* Schooner – near **Addison**

1906 (July 4) Ella *G Eells*, Schooner - near **Libby Island**

1906 (October 25) *Glenullen*, Schooner - **Machias Bay**

1907 (January 12) *Agnes*, Schooner – **Cranberry Isles**

1907 (January 19) *Maud Malloch*, Schooner – **Otter Point**

1907 (January 24) *Adie*, Brig - **Bar Harbor**

1907 (Aprl 21) *Catherine G Howard*, Schooner –**Sequin Island**

1907 (May 16) *Ellen M Mitchell*, Schooner – off **Great Wess Island**

1907 (August 27) *Doris*, Paddle - near **Corea**

1907 (October 8) *Grace Choate*, Schooner – near **Cranberry Island**

Schooner caught in a storm

1908 (March 1) *Waldron Holmes*, Schooner – near **Gouldsboro**

1908 (July 1) *Julia Baker*, Schooner – near **Millbridge**

1908 (August 8) *Three Sisters* – **Baker Island**

1908 (December 1) *Shawmut*, Brigantine - **Machias Bay**

1909 (January 28) *Golden Bell*, Schooner – near **Beals**

1909 (April 22) *Rebecca W Huddell*, Schooner - near **Libby Island**

1909 (May 18) *William G Eadie*, Schooner - near **Gouldsboro**

1910 (November 10) *Mary J Elliot*, Schooner - **Machiasport**

1911 *Tay*, Schooner - Sand Beach in **Acadia National Park**

1911 (July 28) *Almeda Willey*, Schooner – off **Mount Desert**

1912 *Catherine D. Enos*, Fishing vessel – **Isle au Haut**

1912 *New Boxer*, Schooner - **Isle au Haut**

1912 (March 15) *St Leon*, Schooner – near **Corea**

1912 (August 19) *Addie Fuller*, Schooner – off **Cutler**

1913 (February 2) *Emma and Maggie*, Freighter – near **Jonesport**

1913 (March 26) *General Scott*, Schooner – **Quoddy Head**

1913 (April 7) *Thomas Hix*, Schooner – off **Mount Desert**

1913 (July 19) *Yeoman*, Sloop – **Bar Harbor**

1914 (March 4) *Susie and Winnie*, Cargo Ship – **Bar Harbor**

1914 (October 29) *Irvington*, Freighter - **Bar Harbor**

1914 (December 13) *Samuel B Jones*, Freighter - **Machiasport**

1915 (April 3) *Bertha B*, War Ship – near **Long Island**

1915 (May 9) *Fortuna*, Freighter – off **Mount Desert**

1915 (June 2) *Cora Green*, Schooner – **Sequin Island**

Abandon Ship

1915 (September 17) *Lanie Cobb*, Schooner - **West Quoddy Head**

1916 (April) *W E and W L Tuck*, Schooner – near **Baker Island**

1918 ((August 19) *Clement*, Freighter – near **Addison**

1918 (December 30) *Fred B Belano*, Schooner – **Great Wass Island**

1919 (January 22) *Kingsway*, Schooner – near **Lubec**

1919 (October 28) *Rescue*, Freighter – near **Eastport**

1920 *Norumbega*, Steamship - **Southwest Harbor**.

1920 (July 29) *Clara and Mabel*, Schooner – **Mount Desert**

1921 (May 10) *Mabel E Goss*, Schooner - **Sullivan**

1921 (October 5) *Seth Nyman,* Schooner – **Baker Island**

1922 (April 12) *Grace Van Dusen,* , Schooner - **West Quoddy Head**

1923 (April 25) *Kennebec,* Schooner - **Perry**

1923 (August 7) *Diana,* Cargo Ship – **Bar Harbor**

1923 (October 10) *Palm,* Steamer - **Bar Harbor**

1924 (January 26) *Gov. Bodwell,* Freighter – off **Swans Island**

1924 (April 24) *Lewis H St John,* Schooner – near **West Quoddy Head**

1924 (August 6) *Henrietta A Whitney,* Schooner - **Eastport**

1925 (November 28) *John H Meyer.* Brigantine - **Machias Bay**

1926 (August 22) *New York,* Paddle Steamer – off **Corea**

1927 (July 29) *Ara,* Freighter - off **Mount Desert**

1928 (May 7) *Sara Maris,* Schooner – near **Millbridge**

Paddle Steamer *New York*

1931 (January 2) *Angie and Mary,* Freighter – **Sequin Island**

1931 (August 27) *Louise,* Cargo Ship - **Jonesport**

1933(May 8) *Kwasind Refuge* - Motor Yacht – **Ellsworth**

1933(May 8) *Alert Patrika* - Motor Yacht – **Ellsworth**

1933 (December 19) *Moonlight,* Schooner –off **Great Wess Island**

1940 (September 20) *George Gress,* Schooner - **Bar Harbor**

1942 (September 27) *Pofisco,* Freighter – near **Libby Island**

1943 (March 6) *D M Munroe,* Steamer - near **Libby Island**

1944 (December 3) *Cornwallis*, Freighter – off **Mount Desert**

1951 (March 28) *North Star*, Freighter – off **Mount Desert**

1951 (November 13) *Calumet II*, Freighter - **West Quoddy Head Lt**

1957 (November 13) *BC-2596*, Freighter – near **Eastport**

1964 (August) *A G Prentiss*, Freighter – near **Libby Island**

Unknown Wreck lies on the bottom

Machiasport Shipwrecks

Thirty seven known wrecks

"Caledonia" Canadian wreck, schooner
"John C. Myers" American wreck, barque
"GLENULLEN" American wreck, schooner
"Laurissa" Canadian wreck, schooner
"Mabel Purdy" Canadian wreck, schooner
"Mary J. Elliot" American wreck, schooner
"Rebecca W. Huddell" American wreck, schooner
"William Mason" American wreck, schooner
"Seabird" American wreck, schooner
"Sedona" American wreck, schooner
"Shawmut" American wreck,
"Ximena" American wreck, schooner
"Edward W. Murdock" Unidentified wreck
"Scio" American wreck, schooner
"John L. Bowman" American wreck, schooner
"Princeport" Canadian wreck, schooner
"Ella G. Ellis" American? wreck, schooner
"F. C. Lockhart" American? wreck, schooner
"Africa" Canadian wreck, barkentine
"Badjr" American wreck, oil screw
"Samuel B. Jones" American wreck, steam screw
"Florence" British wreck, barque
"D.M. Monroe" American wreck, cargo vessel
"Clearmont" British wreck, barque
"Fame" British wreck

"Eliza Hatfield" Canadian wreck, schooner
"Emma G." Canadian wreck, schooner
"Julia Ellen" Canadian wreck, schooner
"Lizzie B." Canadian wreck, schooner
"Lyra" Canadian wreck, schooner
"Mary E." Canadian wreck, schooner
"Merlin" Canadian wreck, schooner
"Nellie King" Canadian wreck, schooner
"Phoenix" Canadian wreck, schooner
"Playfair" Canadian wreck, schooner –
"Rowena" Canadian wreck, schooner

Stories and Tales

Mount Desert and Downeast

Wreck of the Grand Design

Long Ledge, Mount Desert Island - 1740

The following comes from Cyrus Eaton's 1851 book, *Annals of the town of Warren in Knox County, Maine with the early history of St. Georges, Broadbay and neighboring settlements on the Waldo Patent,* pg. 63 - 65. It provides us with a very graphic picture of the hardships shipwreck survivors faced in uninhabited Maine in the 1700s.

Letters were brought by the Indians from some shipwrecked persons on Mt. Desert, who were suffering every extremity and dying with hunger. The Indians had given them what little aid they could, and now came with letters to this settlement and that at Damariscotta for farther assistance.

Measures were immediately concerted by the people of these two places, and a vessel with provisions dispatched to their relief. They proved to be passengers from the north of Ireland, who had embarked in the ship 'Grand Design,' of two or three hundred tons, bound to Pennsylvania, which was driven ashore and wrecked in a violent storm.

Most of them were persons of wealth and distinction who were going to rejoin their friends and connections in that colony. Many of them had with them a train of bond-servants, male and female, all of whom, on landing from the wreck, they immediately released and gave them an equal chance for life with themselves.

After escaping from the wreck, they examined the island and found it uninhabited. Under this discouraging circumstance, they exerted themselves to the utmost to save what provisions and other necessaries they could from the ship.

Exhausted by their efforts and fainting with thirst, numbers of them repaired to a brook to drink, and, overcome by the cooling draught, never rose again.

Making the best shift for shelter and subsistence which their situation would permit, they dispatched a party of one hundred of their most able and vigorous young men to the main land, in hopes of finding a settlement there from whom assistance might be obtained.

Nothing farther was ever seen or heard of this part of their companions. The remainder, waiting for their return, spent many wearisome months of disappointment, exposure and starvation, relieved only by the scanty and uncertain resources which the waves and shore afforded. Many perished of want.

At length a party of Indians visited the Island, and, though without interpreters, a barter was effected of a few articles of food in exchange for clothing and other matters furnished by the sufferers. Among these passengers were a Mrs. Galloway and another lady, who had not been long married when they left Ireland. The former of these brought with her an infant three months old, whom she nursed in this abode of wretchedness, till blood instead of milk followed its emaciated lips.

Her husband gave to the Indians two pieces of fine Irish linen for one duck, which, refusing to taste himself, he reserved exclusively for her. The sufferings of the mother were such as often to extort from the father a wish that the child might breathe its last. Yet both mother and child survived; whilst the father, as also the husband of the other lady, died from exhaustion.

These two women dug graves and buried their own husbands, there being no men of strength enough remaining to afford any assistance. The vessel that came to their relief brought some provisions, but, as she was for some time detained, these were all exhausted, and they arrived at St. George's in a most famishing condition.

Going on shore at Pleasant Point where there was then only one log-house, they were received with all the hospitality the place would afford. Many of them were richly clad with the remnants of their wardrobes which had escaped the wreck; but now in the impatience of hunger they were ready to snatch half roasted potatoes from the ashes into lawn aprons and silk dresses, and devour them without plate, knife, or fork.

Mrs. Galloway had imagined before landing, because burdened with a child that no one would be willing to receive her; but here she found herself provided with a bed, whilst the rest were glad to sleep on the floor and in hovels as they could.

Before landing, she had inquired what kind of people were settled here, and, hearing they were Irish, exclaimed "alas! I sha'nt be able to speak to them, for I don't know a single word of the Irish language."

She was now rejoiced to find the inhabitants as ignorant of that language as herself, being all from the north of Ireland and of Scottish descent. Sixteen of these persons went to the settlement up the river, the rest to Pemaquid, Sheepscot and Damariscotta. Archibald Gamble, a young man from Ireland, who had then taken a farm in the Upper town, (now the Bucklin lot,) offered himself to Mrs. Galloway, and Mr. McCarter to her companion before mentioned.

Having lost their husbands, whose relations they were going to join in Pennsylvania, and having no acquaintances there themselves, these two women, whose sufferings had bound them together in the closest ties of friendship, accepted their respective offers and remained in the settlement.

The child of Mrs. Galloway was sent for by his uncle in Pennsylvania, who had taken offence at the mother for marrying again so soon, but she declined the offer till he should grow up to determine for himself. He was afterwards lost at sea.

HMS *Halifax* - 1775

She was a schooner built for merchant service at Halifax, Nova Scotia in 1765 and purchased in 1768 by the British Royal Navy for coastal patrol in North America in the years just prior to the American Revolution. She is one of the best documented schooners from early North America.

Captured John Hancock's Ship

In 1769 the *HMS Halifax* confiscated and towed the schooner *Liberty*, later HMS *Liberty*, belonging to John Hancock.

Schooner going down

After an active career on the coast on North America she was wrecked on 15 February 1775 at Foster Island near Machias, Maine. It was reportedly intentionally run aground by a local pilot. The wreck played a role in the Battle of Machias later that year, where its guns were ordered to be recovered by Admiral Samuel Graves.

New York – 1826

Fire at Sea

The Steam Brig left Portland with a crew of eighteen and fourteen passengers aboard. After one day at sea, August 23, she caught on fire while eight miles off Petit Manan Light.

Captain Harrold ordered the ship be abandoned and all hands landed safely shortly before midnight at Petit Manan. The *New York* was completely consumed by the flames and sank to the bottom of the sea.

Sarah – 1835

Mistaken Identity

The packet *Sarah* sailed on its regular run from Boston bound for Eastport, Maine. It would never make it as the master, Captain Pierce, mistook Mount Desert Rock Lighthouse for the flash of Moose Peak Light and wrecked his ship on rocks off Jonesport.

The ballad "The Loss of the Sarah" was written to memorialize the sad event. Two of the verses follow.

Ye landsmen all, now pray draw near,
a lamentation ye shall hear;
A ship was lost at sea
It was Sarah's lot to be.

Thirty two were Sarah's crew
And landsmen were all counted too;
Sixteen survived to reach shore,
Sixteen were lost, they are no more

Schooner NEPTUNE'S BRIDE – 1860

Schooner Wrecks on Malcomb's Ledge -
Another Thirteen Lives Lost !

WRECK OF THE SCHOONER NEPTUNE'S BRIDE.

Rockland, Maine, Sept. 24, 1860.

The schooner *Neptune's Bride*, Capt. JACOB OLSEN, of Gloucester, returning from a successful cruise to the eastward, was caught in the storm of Thursday last, at about ten p.m., while jogging along under foresail, and ran on Malcomb's Ledge, between Seal Island and the Wooden Ball.

The captain and eleven hands were lost in the surf in attempting to land in a boat immediately after she struck.

Two men were left on board the vessel, which bilged in half an hour, filled and worked off into deep water. The men then took the masts, and one was washed off and drowned early in the morning. The survivor, JOSEPH MARSH, of Gloucester, was taken at 5 p.m. Friday.

It was reported here today that one of the twelve men capsized in the surf regained the boat, and was picked up and taken to Isle de Hault. Lost Crew Members:

> JACOB OLSEN, master.
> GEORGE NORWOOD.
> MANUEL SILVA.
> J. ENOS SILVA.
> WILLIAM JOHNSON.
> JAMES BIRD.
> TOLEF ANDERSON.
> WILLIAM HALE.
> J. ANTOINE SILVA.
> PETER JOHNSON.

Young man whose name could not be learned. The schooner was owned by Charles Parkhurst. It was valued at $5,000; insured for $3,500. HENRY JOHNSON, was the man who regained the boat, and was rescued.

Banner of Liberty Middletown New York 1860-09-26

Bar Harbor Ferry Boat Disaster, 1899

Twenty drowned while boarding the ferry,

Two hundred excursionists fell in a mass into the water. The ferry gangplank gave way. The Victims, shut in on all sides, having no avenue of escape, clutched one another and sank in groups before the work of rescue could be begun.

Bar Harbor, ME Aug 6, 1899. At least twenty persons were drowned to-day at Mount Desert Ferry, eight miles from here, by the breaking of a gangplank on which they were walking from the wharf to a steamer which was to have conveyed them to this place. They were members of an excursion party from Bangor and other points on the line of the Maine Central Railroad.

Where the train meets the ferry

They Maine Central Railroad operated it's crack Pullman train, The Bar Harbor Express from New York City and Boston to their dock at Ferry Point in the town of Hancock, Me, 8 miles away across the bay from Bar Harbor. Guests and their luggage would detrain and board the local ferry steamer for the short trip to their summer destination. The dock was connected to the ferry boat by a wooden boarding ramp which had a series of chains and counterweights in order to align the boat deck with the dock at whatever stage the tide was at that moment. The first few guests boarded easily then, when a mass of humanity estimated to be 200 people were on the gangplank at the same time, when it suddenly gave way plunging most into the cold waters of the bay 15 ft below.

Penned in on 3 sides by the pilings of the dock and on the fourth by the boat, they fought for their lives for a few minutes while more than a hundred excursionists above on the dock looked on, stupified, and failing at first to realize the enormity of the tragedy they were witnessing. Ropes and life preservers were thrown to the crowd in the water but a mass panic ensued. Clinging to each other some eventually slipped beneath the surface to drown. Many persons taken alive from the water were unconscious and near death. Many of those were revived with great difficulty.

The steamer *Cymbria,* also owned by the Maine Central Railroad made a quick trip from Bar Harbor with 4 doctors aboard. Rescuers struggled to save those they could but it was nearly impossible to get into the spot with small boats. Many were pulled out of the water by ropes and manpower. Those needing immediate medical attention were taken to the nearby Hotel Bluffs where the doctors had set up emergency facilities.

The freight house at the dock was turned into an emergency morgue, the bodies being moved there for identification as soon as they were removed from the water. By noon 17 bodies had arrived there and 3 more, being taken to Bar Harbor on the steamer Sappho, died while enroute for an appalling death toll of twenty citizens.

Coroner D. L. Field of Ellsworth, Me has impaneled a jury to hold an inquest. The jury will begin its work in the morning. After the bodies in the freight house had been identified, coroner Field gave the necessary permission to have them moved, and relatives and friends soon after took each in charge and returned them to their respective homes for burial.

Taken from the archives of the New York Times

Ferry *Cimbria* – 1899

Aground on Mount Desert Island

The *Cimbria* was a ferry run by the Bangor and Bar Harbor line. She was 289.14 tons, 116.7 feet long, 18.5 foot beam, 7 draught, and 500 horse power and made her maiden voyage in Brewer in 1882. She ran from Bangor to Bar Harbor. She also made some runs down the Penobscot River to Belfast. One day she ran aground at Mount Desert point due to foggy

Cimbria on rocks at Mount Desert

conditions, but was not severely ruined. After being hauled off the rocks, she was modernized before heading back to her launch. As railroad travel became more popular the *Cimbria* relocated, in 1915 to Bridgeport, Connecticut then in 1920 to Chicago. The 1922 register listed *Cimbria* as abandoned.

Alice M. Davenport - 1902

Wreck saved by a revolver

19 August 1902 – The schooner *Alice M. Davenport*, which was wrecked off Seal Island ledges a week ago, was raised using pontoons. However the pontoons failed and she immediately sank again in 120 feet of water.

The 'King of Seal Island' Captain W. F. Hill said, "Monday night about 6:15, we were snug in my camp on Seal Island. There were seven of my men, my wife and myself. It was so thick outside that one could not see five yards ahead.

Suddenly my four watch dogs began to bark and we knew that there was trouble near the ledges. We all ran out and going to what we call Myrrh Cove, could just discern the bowsprit of a vessel sticking up over the ledges.

Three masted schooner flounders

We could hear excited cries aboard and jumped into our dories and pulled out. We found a three-masted schooner fast on the ledges, her stern awash and with a bad list to port.

"It was so dark that we couldn't see, but could hear the crew shouting on deck. We cried out to them and we could hear a woman's voice asking that she be taken off. There was a heavy sea on and we had difficulty in keeping the dories by the vessel. I boarded the schooner, which proved to be the *Alice M. Davenport*, and found the crew the most excited set of men I have ever seen in my life.

The woman proved to be Miss McKown, the daughter of the captain, and I consented to take her ashore. The vessel was not over 100 yards from the island. Miss McKown was lowered into the dory and was rowed ashore. They didn't know where they were and reckoned that it must be Isle au Haut.

"The first inquiry of the young lady was: 'Is there a woman on this island?' and I assured her by introducing her to my wife. Such an affecting scene between two women I've never seen in my whole existence and her joy of finding one of her own sex on such a barren island in the Atlantic knew no bounds.

Then we set about rescuing the belongings of the captain and crew and brought everything ashore that wasn't screwed down. We got ashore all of the provisions and furniture. Then came such a deluge of rain as if the heaven had opened its flood gates upon us.

"The *Davenport* began to pound on the rocks and almost turned turtle. We ran a line ashore and made her fast and the crew and Captain McKown came to my camp. I don't exactly own a hotel, but we had 21 people in our camp that night and I stowed them away as best I could.

"Poor old Captain McKown broke down and cried like a child when he met his daughter in the camp. He had $5,000 in the *Davenport,* with $2,000 insurance. He had set his whole heart on this vessel and loved her as a father would his child. He could not account for the accident except that the schooner had gotten away from him. She was new and he was unused to her. He had sailed side by side for miles that day with a son on another schooner, and had lost track of him.

"The next day Captain McKown set out in his launch for Vinalhaven, to notify the owners of the disaster and I was put in charge. Going away he gave me his revolver and I was placed in charge of the *Davenport*.

It was not long before a fleet of five or six sloops were seen coming up from Long Island with an unusual number of men on them. They drew up alongside the *Davenport* and the men began to clamber up the sides to the deck, in order to loot the vessel I suppose.

Get off this ship

"Get back there,' I shouted. Don't put a foot on the deck of this vessel.' Save for the first mate, who was below, I was alone. They didn't heed my warning and one of them had his hands on the rail ready to spring over, when I drew my revolver and pointing it at him said, 'if you put your foot over that rail you are a dead man.' and I'd shoot too.'

The revolver did the business and they went back into their boats, and finally seeing that I meant business sailed for home."

The New York Times, New York, NY 20, August 1902

Schooner ANNIE GUS - 1905

Schooner hits Freeman's Rock.

Captain and Crew of the *Annie Gus* Escape to Great Wass Island.

JONESPORT. Me., April 2.---The little coasting schooner Annie Gus, commanded by Capt. Charles Berry of Machiasport, which left Calais on Friday with a cargo of lumber for Providence, met a heavy northwesterly gale off Moose Peak Light to-day and in running into Mud Hole Channel for a harbor struck on Freeman's Rock and will probably prove a total loss.

It is reported that her captain and crew of three men, who were also from Machiasport, reached Great Wass Island in safety in their own boat after a hard row of two miles against the wind.

The New York Times, New York, NY 3 Apr 1905

Great Storms

on the Coast of Maine

The Storm of 1842.

On Wednesday afternoon, November 30, 1842, a snow storm began, which turned to rain about nine o'clock in the evening. The wind had blown moderately through the day, but when night came on it increase until it blew with great violence from the east-southeast, shifting to the east-northeast at two o'clock in the morning, when it quickly subsided.

In some parts, a great deal of snow fell, and travel on the railroads was greatly obstructed, fifteen inches of snow being on the ground the next day at Dover, N. H. The storm began early in the morning as far south as Washington and Baltimore, and much snow fell there. The temperature was also low, being at Belfast, Maine, on the day before only six degrees above zero, the coldest November day that had been known there for several years.

Ships Caught in a Blizzard

At Boston, the storm was much more severe than at any other port in that vicinity. Many vessels were anchored in the harbor when the storm came on, and they were driven from their moorings, being either jammed against each other or the wharves. They were badly chafed and broken, and several of them were sunk. In the very heart of the city the sound of falling masts and of vessels crashing together was heard from time to time above the noise of the storm. It was deemed dangerous to go to the end of the wharves lest some large craft might dash against them, carrying them away. In the night, several sailors were drowned.

Among the many wrecks caused by the storm in the few short hours it continued were two or three that made it memorable.

One of them was that of the bark Isadore, a new and beautiful vessel of four hundred tons burden, commanded and owned by Capt. Leander Foss. This was its first trip, and it sailed on the morning of the storm from Kennebunk, Maine, for New Orleans.

In the blinding snow and the tempest of that night the craft was driven on a point of rocks near Cape Neddock, Maine, called Bald head, and wrecked. The entire crew of fifteen belonged in Kennebunkport, and all perished. Five were fathers of families, and left in all twenty children. Two were young men, the only sons of widows.

The schooner Napoleon, commanded by Capt. James York, sailed from Calais, Maine, for New York, with a cargo of lumber, on the twenty-eighth of the month. The gale struck the vessel out in the ocean on the night of the storm and carried away both masts.

Wreck Covered in Ice

She capsized and righted, but was filled with water. The cook, a Scotch lad, was probably lost when the vessel went over, as he was not seen again. The others of the crew remained on deck, in the cold and darkness and tempest, and one after another they lay down and died. The craft was driven about by the mighty wind, but where no one knew or cared.

The next day and another night passed away. Death was what they desired, and all but one of them found it. When the wreck had reached a point about forty miles south of Monhegan, it fell in with the schooner Echo of Thomaston, Maine.

Captain York had survived until within and hour or two of their meeting with the Echo, and when the captain of that vessel came on board the wreck only the mate was found alive, he being badly frozen. The other six had all died, and their bodies had been washed away except that of one man, which was jammed in among the lumber in such a manner that it could not be extricated without great danger.

The saddest wreck caused by the storm was that of the schooner James Clark, of sixty tons burden, belonging in St. John, N. B., commanded and owned by Captain Beck. It was on a trip from St. John to Boston, and there were twenty persons on board.

They left Portland on the morning of the storm, and late that afternoon were driven ashore at Rye beach, the vessel becoming a total wreck. At six o'clock in the evening, which was soon after the vessel struck, the cabin was stove in, and the people were compelled to remain on deck.

The heavy sea dashed over them, and they were washed from one side of the vessel to the other, their clothing being torn off from them. They suffered intensely from the exposure to cold and water, and some died, the first being Mrs. Margaret Stewart's six month's old baby boy, named Willie, who expired in her arms. She had wrapped him so closely for protection from exposure that his death was probably hastened thereby.

The mother became insensible and when rescued was found among some lumber almost covered with water. Her arms were stiffened in the position in which she had held her child, and remained so for some time after arriving at the land. She was saved, however, to mourn the loss of her boy.

Mrs. Mary Hebersen, a widow of about fifty, accompanied by her daughter Hannah, who was twelve years old, was on her way to an aunt's in Holden, Mass. For hours they kept together in their hopeless condition as well as the waves would permit. At length the daughter, becoming benumbed with cold, lay down upon the deck at her mother's feet and died.

While she lay there, her life fast ebbing away, her mother watched over her, and raising her eyes to heaven commended her daughter's spirit to her Maker. This excellent mother was no sooner apprehensive of the death of her daughter than she forgot the tempest and laid herself down by the side of her child. In fifteen minutes her spirit also had fled.

As soon as it was possible, one of the sailors took a long rope, fastened one end of it on the deck, and jumped into the raging surf with the other end tied to him. He fought his way to the shore, and by means of the rope the captain and crew and ten of the passengers, five women, two men, a girl and a boy, and a child sixteen months old, were saved.

Only one person, Dennis Mahaney, perished while attempting to reach the shore on the rope. Mrs. Hebersen and Mr. Mahaney were the only adults lost, the rest being children. Five bodies were recovered.

Those most instrumental in saving these people were a Mr. Yeaton and his son, who unweariedly[sic] and at imminent peril of their lives assisted in getting them on shore. But for their efforts many more would have perished. Mr. Yeaton's family generously placed everything they had at the disposal of the sufferers.

They gave them the use of the whole house and freely distributed their extra clothing among them, both mariners and passengers having lost theirs, except what they wore when rescued, some of them being nearly naked.

Historic Storms of New England, its Gales, Hurricanes, Tornadoes, Showers with Thunder and Lightning, Great Snow Storms, Rains, Freshets, Floods, Droughts, Cold Winters, Hot Summers, Avalanches, Earthquakes, Dark Days, etc..., by Sidney Perley, 1891, pages 289-291

The Portland Storm - 1898

Steamer *PORTLAND* SUNK; 118 LIVES LOST.

STEAMER FROM BOSTON WRECKED SUNDAY OFF CAPE COD WENT DOWN IN THE STORM. THIRTY-FOUR BODIES OF PASSENGERS SO FAR RECOVERED.

NEWS TAKEN TO BOSTON BY A SPECIAL COURIER, TELEGRAPHIC COMMUNICATION BEING IMPOSSIBLE.

Boston, Mass., Nov. 29. -- The steamer *Portland*, bound from Boston to Portland, went down off Truro, on the outside of Cape Cod, Sunday morning. Every man, woman, and child on board at the time of the disaster was drowned, in all 118.

Steamer Portland

The list of those on board include fifty-one passengers and forty-eight officers and crew.

NONE LIVES TO TELL.
The *Portland* left Boston on Saturday evening and was last seen afloat by a fisherman in the vicinity of Thacher's Island several hours later. Nobody knows what happened in the awful hours on the angry sea which followed, and the lips that might tell the tale are sealed in death.

The surmise is that with the wind blowing a gale at the rate of seventy miles an hour, a rate which has never been equaled except once before in the written history of weather along this coast, with the waves running to mighty heights, the steamer became disabled and was swept by the raging seas across the entrance to Massachusetts Bay and down upon the graveyard of Cape Cod. The *Portland*, with its side paddlewheels and large exposure of hull, must have been smashed by the seas and rolled by the mad waves, and at last foundered in the height of the gale Sunday morning.

The news of the disaster is meager because of blockaded railroads and fallen telegraph wires. The only additional facts brought from Cape Cod by a courier, who was thirty-two hours making the journey, is that vast quantities of wreckage of the Portland and thirty-four bodies have been cast upon the beach at Truro.

The first discovery of the disaster was made by Surfman Bowley of the High Head Life Saving station, who found on the beach the body of a negro encircled by a life belt of the steamer *Portland*. Soon after bodies were washed ashore and recovered by the life-saving crews of the three stations in the vicinity. Not a glimpse of the steamer was obtained by the life savers. The destruction of the vessel was complete, as hundreds of barrels, boxes, and other articles of freight attest. From just east of the Peaked Hill Bar Station to the High Head Station, three miles eastward, the shore is heaped with debris.

The *Portland* carried a miscellaneous cargo of 100 tons of merchandise.

The vessel was built in Bath in 1890, and was a side-wheel steamer of 1,517 tons net burden. Her length is 230 feet, beam 42, depth 15 feet. She was valued at $250,000 and is fully insured.

WRECKAGE 15 MILES SOUTH.
Dr. Maurice Richardson of Beacon Street, this city, has been at his Summer home at Wellfleet during the storm, and his story corroborates the early accounts of the loss of the *Portland*, for he saw two of the bodies washed ashore and on them were life preservers marked with the vessel's name. Dr. Richardson was on the first train from Cape Cod which arrived in this city late to-night. To take the train he was obliged to ride fifteen miles.

"I saw two of the bodies picked up," said Dr. Richardson. "One was probably that of a deckhand, a man of about twenty. He had on a life preserver marked '*PORTLAND*.' The other body was that of a stout woman. She, too, wore a life belt with the steamer's name on it.

Wreckage is coming ashore for fifteen miles along the coast. I picked up three piano keys and a piano cage ashore, but, of course, I don not know that they were from the *Portland*. Among the wreckage was a large quantity of furniture upholstered in red plush. Then there were cased of lard directed to *Portland*."

"I was fifteen miles south of High Head. There is nothing in the fact that wreckage was found so far south to contradict the report that it was at High Head that the *Portland* struck, for the current runs south along the shore."

Dr. Richardson said he had heard one theory advanced that the *Portland* had foundered far to the north, somewhere near Cape Ann, and that all the wreckage and bodies had drifted across the bay to Cape Cod. He said that at Orleans the body of a girl of about twenty was found. She had a gold watch and a ring marked "J.G.E." Her watch stopped at 9:17. The double wheel of the *Portland* came ashore at Orleans.

The insurance upon the hull of the *Portland* was placed in Boston, partly in the Boston Marine Insurance Company and partly through the Boston office of Johnson & Higgins. It was valued at about $200,000. The insurance upon the cargo of the steamer, which consisted of dry goods, boots and shoes, flour, &c., was placed in New York and amounted to $45,000.

The New York Times New York 1898-11-30

Spreading the News - Orleans to France to New York to Boston

The storm severed telegraph and electric lines knocking out all communications in the area making it difficult to get news of the *Portland* to Boston. The problem was solved by sending a wire to France over the trans-Atlantic French cable from the station in Orleans. From there the news was wired back to New York over another cable and then telegraphed to Boston.

42 Maine Vessels Lost or Damaged in the *Portland Gale*

- Addie Sawyer (schooner), Calais, ME
- Africa, Portland, ME
- Alida (schooner), White Head, ME ~ *While lying in Islesboro, gale sprang up, parting her anchor chains and driving her to sea. Blown along for some 20 miles, finally fetching up on the flats at Lobster Cove. Crew reached shore without difficulty.*Anna W. Barker (schooner), White Head, ME / Sedgwick, ME ~ *Wrecked on Southern Island, 3 miles from station. Crew escaped without injury.*
- B.R. Woodside (schooner), Boston Bay / Bath, ME
- Bertha E. Glover (schooner), Vineyard Sound / Rockland, ME

- Carrie C. Miles, Portland, ME
- Cathie C. Berry (schooner), Vineyard Sound / Eastport, ME
- Champion (brig), Quoddy Head, ME / 6 ~ *Wrecked near the Quoddy Head station, but her crew succeeded in reaching shore in their own boat.*
- Charles J. Willard (schooner), Quoddy Head, ME / Portland, ME ~ *While lying at anchor in West Quoddy Bay, a gale sprang up and her chains parted. She soon stranded and her crew was helped by life-savers and local fishermen.*
- Clara Leavitt (schooner), Gay Head, MA / Portland, ME / 7 ~ *Stranded the morning of November 27 and didn't last an hour. Breakers swept over her heavily as the crew took to the rigging. Her deck house was destroyed in 20 minutes and all three masts fell when the weather shrouds slackened. Six lives were lost.*

Sailing Ship on the bottom

- David Faust (schooner), Nantucket / Ellsworth, ME
- D.T. Pachin (schooner), Cape Ann / Castine, ME
- E.G. Willard (schooner), Vineyard Sound/ Rockland, ME
- Ella Frances (schooner), Cape Cod / Rockland, ME
- Ellis P. Rogers (schooner), Cape Ann / Bath, ME
- F.H. Smith (schooner), Cape Cod / New Haven, ME
- Fannie May, Rockland, ME
- Forest Maid (schooner), Portsmouth, NH / Portland, ME
- Fred A. Emerson (downeast lumberman), Boston Bay

- Georgietta (schooner), White Head, ME ~ *Stranded on Spruce Head Island during the heavy gale and snowstorm. In attempting to haul her off, the foremast and main topmast were carried away.*
- Grace (schooner), Cape Cod / Ellsworth, ME
- Idella Small (schooner) Portland. ME *Driven ashore by the gale on the east side of Davis Neck. As she took bottom one of her crew jumped ashore and sought help at the station. Two others on board safely off. On the next high tide after she went ashore, the vessel drifted up on the beach at Bay View and became a total wreck.*
- Ivy Bell (schooner), Jerrys Point, NH / Damariscotta, ME/ 4 ~ *Dragged ashore near the entrance to Portsmouth Harbor. All crewmen taken off safely.*
- J.M. Eaton (schooner), Cape Ann / Gloucester, ME
- James A. Brown (schooner), Vineyard Sound / Thomaston, ME

> **FAST ON ROCKS.**
> Steamer Fairfax on Sow and Pigs Shoals.
> All Night Battling With the Gale, Bound to Boston.

- Jordon L. Mott (schooner), Wood End, MA / Rockland, ME / Capt. Dyer/5 ~ *One life lost when she sank at her anchor in Provincetown Harbor the early morning of November 27. Four men, who were quickly approaching collapse after having been in the shrouds for 15 hours, crept down from the rigging as the life-savers arrived. The lifeless body of the captain's father was lashed in the rigging.*
- Lester A. Lewis (schooner), Wood End, MA / Bangor, ME / 5 ~ *Sank in Provincetown Harbor the early morning of November 27. Her crew took refuge in the rigging, where they perished before help could arrive.*

- Lillian, Portland, ME
- Lucy A. Nickels (bark), Point Allerton, MA / Searsport, ME / 5 ~ *Wrecked by the hurricane on Black Rock. In attempting to swim to the rock, the master and mate was drowned. The other members of the crew found in a gunning hut on the rock. The vessel was a wreck and one of the survivors seriously injured.*
- Lucy Hammond (schooner), Vineyard Sound / Machias, ME
- Lunet (schooner), Naushon Island, MA / Calais, ME
- Marion Draper (schooner), Vineyard Sound / Bath, ME
- Nellie Doe (schooner), Vineyard Sound / Bangor, ME

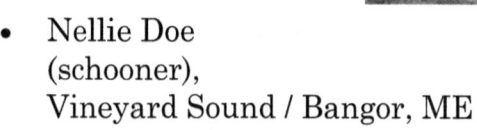

Albert Butler

- Neptune, Portland, ME
- Queen of the West (schooner), Fletcher's Neck, ME / 2 ~ *Wrecked on Fletchers Neck. Both crewmen and a dog brought off safely.*
- Rendo, Portland, ME
- Rienzi (schooner), Cape Ann / Sedgwick, ME
- S.F. Mayer, Rockland, ME
- Silver Spray, Portland, ME
- Sloop (unknown), White Head, ME
- T.W. Cooper (schooner), Portsmouth, NH / Machias, ME

Resource:

A Naval History of the American Revolution, 1912

Bangor Daily News

ageofpirates.com

Biddeford Daily Journal.

Brooksville Buildings and Sites on the National Historic Register

Castine Historical Society

Coastal Pilot

Dane York, "A History and Stories of Biddeford", Mc Arthur Library

Elaine Jones (Maine Department of Marine Resources).

Edward Rowe Snow, "Great Storms and Shipwrecks off the New England Coast".

Eyewitness Accounts of the American Revolution, 1779 Reprint (New York: The New York Times and Arno press, 1971).

John Perry Fish "Unfinished Voyages: A Chronical of Shipwrecks".

Jeffrey A. Scully, "It Happened Right Here," McArthur Library,

Joseph Smith, "Gleanings From the Sea."

Light House Digest

Lighthouses of the Maine Coast, Robert Thayer Sterling, 1935

Maine Historic Archaeological Sites Inventory

Maine Historic Preservation Commission

Nat'l Geographic Maps

Old Orchard Mirror

Rodney Laughton, "Images of America – Scarborough"

Space.com

The Friends of Wood Island Lighthouse

Treasure Cache.net

WreckHunters.net

Johnson, *General History of the Pyrates*

Daniel A. Williams, "Early *American Literature"*

Colman, *It is a Fearful Thing,*

Mather, *The Vial Poured Out upon the Sea*

Linebaugh and Rediker, *The Many-Headed Hydra*

Hugh F. Rankin, *The Golden Age of Piracy*

J.M. Beattie, *Crime and the Courts in England, 1660-1800*

Archibald Hamilton to Secretary Stanhope, June 12, 1716, Colonial Office papers (CO) 137/12, f. 19, Public Record Office, London

"Trial of Thomas Davis," Oct. 28, 1717,

Privateering and Piracy in the Colonial Period: Illustrative Documents (New York, 1923),

The Tryals of Major Stede Bonnet and Other Pirates (London, 1719)

W. Noel Sainsbury *et al.*, eds., *Calendar of State Papers, Colonial Series, America and the Wes*

Boston News-Letter, Aug. 15, 1720.

Rediker, "The Seaman as Spirit of Rebellion: Authority, Violence, and Labor Discipline at Sea," in *Between the Devil and the Deep Blue Sea*

Boston News-Letter, Nov. 14, 1720;

"Proceedings of the Court held on the Coast of Africa," High Court of Admiralty papers (HCA) 1/99, f. 101, Public Record Office, London

George Francis Dow and John Henry Edmonds, The *Pirates of the New England Coast, 1630-1730*

G.T. Crook, ed., *The Complete Newgate Calendar*

Boston Gazette, Oct. 24-31, 1720

Expedition Whydah, by Barry Clifford with Paul Perry

Finding New England's Shipwrecks and Treasure, by Robert Ellis Cahill

tinpan.fortunecity.com

Treasure Wreck: The Fortunes and Fate of the Pirate Ship Whydah,

Boston Globe, August 24, 1986 and June 2, 1006.

Cordingly, David. *Under the Black Flag..*

Ellms, Charles. The Project Gutenberg eBook, *The Pirates Own Book*

William Bradford - *Of Plymouth Plantation, 1620-1647*

Defoe, Daniel. *The General History of the Pyrates.* Dover

cindyvallar.com/

CapeCodLinks.com

NationalGeographic.com

piratesoul.com

National Maritime Museum, London

Maine Lighthouses: Documentation of Their Past, J. Candace Clifford and Mary Louise Clifford, 2005.

Annual Report of the Light House Board, various years.

The Statutes at Large and Treaties of the United States of America...,Volume 9, 1851.

Frommer's New England, Lisa M. Legarde, Dale Northrup, 1996.

History of the state of Maine, Volume 1, Maine Historical Society, 1869.

thefreedictionary.com

*A new Universal Gazetteer, or, Geographical Dictionary: Containing...*Jedidiah Morse, 1821.

U-Boat.net

Sailors' Narratives of Voyages Along the New England Coast, 1514-1624, Notes by George Parker Winship, 1905.

Books by Ted Burbank

- Pirates and Treasure in New England
- Shipwrecks, Pirates and Treasure on Cape Cod
- A Homeowner's Complete Guide to Energy Independence
- The "Islands" of Ocean Bluff and Brant Rock
- 365 Ways to Unplug Your Kids or *How to have fun without TV or Computers*
- A Guide to Plymouth's Famous Burial Hill
- A Cookbook for UNLUCKY Fishermen or *How to Cook Bait* – by Kenneth Burbank

Need an entertaining speaker?

Ted is available to provide a presentation on any of the subjects covered by his books (except maybe "How to Cook Bait) and/or participant in your pirate festival.

Ted Burbank

Call: 508.794.1200 to schedule

www.ingramcontent.com/pod-product-compliance
Lightning Source LLC
Chambersburg PA
CBHW071310110426
42743CB00042B/1241